D0205865

Open Road's Best of
Walt Disney World
& Orlando
by Lisa Addison
Open Road Travel Guides –
Guiding You to the Best in Travel!

PHOTO CREDITS

The following photos are from wikimedia commons: p. 9: Juliancolton; p. 77: neuro: p. 78: Justin DiPierro; p. 80: cburnett; p. 109: Imagempt; p. 111: Peter Dutton; p. 144: Krismast;.

The following photos are from flickr.com: front cover: nsaplayer; p. 1: edanley; p. 3: Raymond Brown; p. 5: txbowen; pp. 8, 154 top: RichardBH; p. 10: Raymond Brown; p. 11: sanctumsolitude; pp. 14, 73, 106: Joe Shlabotnik; pp. 18, 33 right, 36, 44 bottom, 62: PrincessAshley; p. 20: Definitely Disney; p. 22: adactio; p. 24: milan.boers; p. 25: Barnyard BBS; p. 28: hyku; pp. 29, 46: anne.oeldorfhirsch; p. 30 left: James Ellsworth; p. 30 right: Andrew Galloway; p. 31 left, 32, 37, 38, 41 bottom, 51, 63, 64, 65 right, 66: JoshMcConnell; p. 31 right: marada; pp. 33, 58: The Consortium; pp. 34 right, 52, 69 right, 71, 130: ckramer; p. 35: CP; p. 39: Seamy Underbelly; p. 40: Occam; p. 41 top: coconut wireless; p. 45 top: Theme Park Mom; pp. 47, 72: daryl_mitchel; pp. 2 top, 48, 53, 125: sanctumsolitude; p. 49 top: Greencolander; p.49 bottom: HGruber; p. 50: Joe Shlabotnik; pp. 54, 86: lemoncat1; p. 55: n2linux; p. 56: 2Eklectick; p 57: Thomas_Jung; p. 59: tom.arthur; p. 61: qwrrty; p. 65 left: Evan Wohrman; p. 67: dbking; p. 68 left: matt44053; p. 68 right: davef3138; p. 69 left: aharden; p. 70: Definitely Disney; p. 83: Sam Howzit; p. 84: divemasterking2000; p. 85: Paul Mannix; p. 103: hyku; pp. 104, 107: LancerE; p. 105: vcalzone; p. 112: Penny Higgins; pp. 119, 143: finna dat; p. 127: tequilamike; p. 128: gbrunett; p. 129: James Ellsworth; p. 137: ConspiracyofHappiness; p. 138: Loren Javier; p. 139: Salt of the Earth.

The following photo is from Jonathan Stein: back cover, p. 17.

Open Road Publishing
P.O. Box 284, Cold Spring Harbor, NY 11724
www.openroadguides.com

ISBN 13: 978-1-59360-206-2
Library of Congress Control No. 2015915680

For photo credits see psge 2.

CONTENTS

Maps
Orlando area 13
Disney World Resort & Environs 26-27
Orlando area 74-75
Universal & International Drive area 81
Orlando Driving map 119
Disney Railroad & Monorail 121

I. Introduction

Sun-drenched Orlando captivates visitors with great theme parks (**Walt Disney World** of course!) and attractions; superb shopping; cultural and historical venues; outdoor adventures; thrilling water parks; diverse dining; entertainment and nightlife; and more. There's no getting around the fact that Disney is the main reason that many families make the trek to this city again and again. But there are lots of other things here worth seeing and doing as well.

Naturally, we'll give you all of the information you need on the world-famous parks - where you can ride coasters, get splashed on adventure rides, feel like a kid again, and let your imagination run wild. Walt Disney World - the playground for all ages - opened in 1971 with just one theme park, the **Magic Kingdom**. Now, there are four major parks, two waterparks, resort hotels, restaurants, shops, and so much more. How big is WDW? Around 40 square miles – twice the size of Manhattan.

Interestingly, although WDW keeps things fresh and Disney Imagineers and producers are continually choreographing new shows and parades, sometimes replacing an entire attraction, and revamping theme rides, much of it remains the same. Perhaps that's why generations of families return again and again to rekindle fond memories and make some new ones too.

But **Orlando** has a few other things up its sleeves besides theme parks. In addition to Disney, we'll also clue you in on Orlando's other must-see attractions and cultural gems, plus the area's best dining, top spots to shop and the hottest shows in town.

If you're looking for a place where you can have fun in the sun while making memories to last a lifetime, Orlando is the right place. Just make sure you pack the sunscreen because it's a hot destination in more ways than one!

2. Overview

If you've never been to Orlando or spent time at Walt Disney World, you might wonder what all the hoopla is about. Why do people get so exited about a theme park? Well, therein lies part of the answer. It's not just a theme park. There's something a bit magical about Disney.

Sure, there are those who complain about the crowds, all of the baby strollers, and that there are kids everywhere you turn. But you have to wonder about people who seem surprised that there are so many children at a place that has attractions with names like **Mad Tea Party** and **Dumbo the Flying Elephant**! This place was made for kids.

But that doesn't mean that Disney is just for kids or families. You'll hear this a lot but there really is something here for everyone - even if you don't believe in magic or fairy dust. And even if you hate strollers.

MAGIC KINGDOM

Step inside the Magic Kingdom and you'll experience what many think is the actual essence of Disney magic. In the more than three decades since it opened, the Magic Kingdom has remained sort of the king of the hill when it comes to theme parks. And even after all this time it still draws **more yearly visitors** than any other theme park.

It can be confusing but you'll soon get the hang of the layout. The **Magic Kingdom** sits on 107 acres and is divided into five areas, or "lands" – **Tomorrowland**, **Fantasyland**, **Frontierland**, **Liberty Square** and **Adventureland**. Each land has a theme and maintaining that theme is part of what makes things click here.

There are certain rides that have retained their popularity year after

year and appeal to all ages. A few are **Splash Mountain**, **Pirates of the Caribbean**, **Jungle Cruise**, **Space Mountain**, and **Haunted Mansion**. If you're already a Disney fan then you've likely been on all of these. Haven't yet joined the Disney bandwagon? Once you visit, you're certain to be back for repeat visits.

EPCOT

Opening in 1982 and conceived by Walt Disney, **Epcot** was to be a place that would "take its cue from the new ideas and new technologies that are now emerging from the creative centers of American industry." But don't get the idea that everything is about technology because the park is also kid-friendly. In fact, there's something cool for kids - "Kidcot" stations at every Epcot venue. At the stations, children can create a free souvenir to take home with them. The more spots they visit, the more they can add to their masterpiece.

The 300-acre park has two themed areas, **Future World** and **World Showcase**. Future World centers on attractions that focus on energy, communication, the land and our environment, the ocean, imagination, transportation and space exploration. The World Showcase highlights the culture, attractions and cuisine of 11 countries. It's where you can learn about Japan, Norway, France, Germany, Morocco and other countries, enjoy unique attractions, and sample cuisine from all of the different countries.

Besides enjoying the wide-open spaces of Epcot, check out popular adventure rides like Soarin' or board the "Living With The Land" boat ride for a tour of greenhouses and fish production. In the evenings, stick around for the show **IllumiNations: Reflections of Earth**, a stunning fireworks, laser and music show that's the perfect way to cap off the Epcot experience. It lasts about 15 minutes and is visible from anywhere around the lagoon.

DISNEY'S HOLLYWOOD STUDIOS

Formerly known as MGM Studios, this park that's devoted to the world of movies and TV shows, opened in 1989 with just a handful of attractions, a few restaurants, and an evening fireworks show. But starting in 1994 when the **Twilight Zone Tower of Terror** attraction opened here, the park got more and more popular.

Other attractions that are a hit include the **Rock 'n' Roller Coaster**, the **Beauty and the Beast** stage show, and the **Fantasmic!** show. **Toy Story Mania!** has become very popular as well (note: the **American Idol experience** has been canceled).

A couple of eateries – **The Hollywood Brown Derby** and **50s Prime**

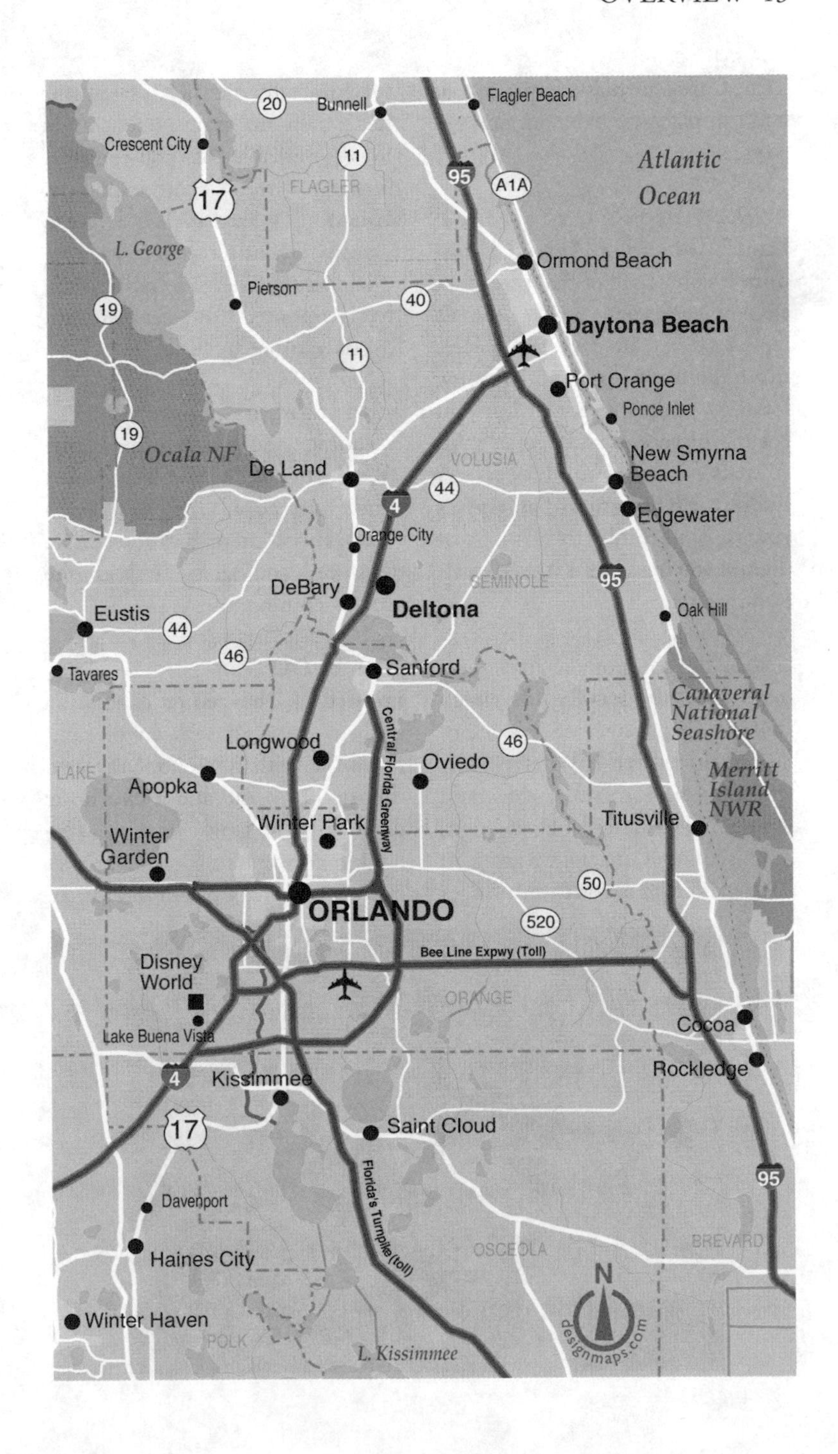

Bunnell
Flagler Beach
Crescent City
Atlantic Ocean
FLAGLER
L. George
Ormond Beach
Pierson
Daytona Beach
Port Orange
Ponce Inlet
Ocala NF
De Land
VOLUSIA
New Smyrna Beach
Edgewater
Orange City
DeBary
Deltona
SEMINOLE
Oak Hill
Eustis
Tavares
Sanford
Canaveral National Seashore
Central Florida Greenway
Longwood
Oviedo
LAKE
Apopka
Merritt Island NWR
Winter Park
Titusville
Winter Garden
ORLANDO
Bee Line Expwy (Toll)
Disney World
ORANGE
Lake Buena Vista
Cocoa
Rockledge
Kissimmee
Saint Cloud
Florida's Turnpike (toll)
Davenport
Haines City
OSCEOLA
BREVARD
Winter Haven
POLK
L. Kissimmee
designmaps.com

Time Cafe – are blasts from the past and fun places to hang out and get a bite to eat.

ANIMAL KINGDOM

Launched in 1998, **Animal Kingdom** is comprised of 500 acres that are home to about 1,700 animals representing 250 different species throughout the park. OK, sorry for the numbers overload but you get the picture - there are a lot of animals wandering this property. A ride on the **Kilimanjaro Safari** gives you the opportunity to see many of them as you travel across the **African Savannah**.

One of the more popular attractions here is the **Kali River Rapids**, which is obviously a water ride. It's one of our favorites but it's pretty tame when it comes to water rides and it doesn't last nearly long enough. Still, it's a lot of fun and we go again and again. If you don't want to get wet (uh, why go on a water ride then?) there are yellow ponchos/rain slickers available that you can wear during the ride. Another popular attraction is **Expedition Everest**, a family-friendly but very exciting roller coaster. There's a mythical yeti that is supposed to be scary but isn't. This is another fun one.

You'll find plenty of restaurants here, including one of our favorites, **Flame Tree Barbecue**. We're salivating just thinking of the pulled pork sandwich we always get there. Rainforest Cafe does well and seems to keep the crowds coming, too.

ORLANDO

Located in the center of Florida midway between Jacksonville and Miami, less than an hour drive to the Atlantic and and **a two-hour drive to Gulf Coast beaches**, Orlando's convenient location makes it the ideal vacation spot in Florida.

The city had humble beginnings, so much so that its founders probably never dreamed it would grow from just two square miles when it was incorporated in 1875.

Some of the "neighborhoods" of Orlando that you might become familiar with when you visit here and enjoy various attractions, restaurants, and entertainment include the following:

Lake Buena Vista: The community of Lake Buena Vista stretches north of Downtown Disney and southeast to the other side of I-4, off Exit 68. This is where most off-site visitors to Disney World stay, and there are also good dining options here.

Universal Orlando Area: An entertainment venue with rides, shopping, eateries, etc (see photo above). A big draw is CityWalk, a very popular destination offering clubs, concert venues, shops, restaurants, and more. With more than a dozen restaurants and the world's largest Hard Rock Cafe, Universal Orlando's CityWalk is a culinary force. At Islands of Adventure, each of the six lands has between two and six eateries – not all of them hamburger joints. To get to Universal, take I-4 Exit 75A from eastbound lanes, Exit 74B when you're westbound.

Kissimmee: Although Orlando is the focus of most theme-park visitors, Kissimmee is actually closer to Walt Disney World. To visit the area, follow I-4 to Exit 64A. Allow about 15 to 25 minutes to travel from WDW, or about 35 minutes from I-Drive.

Celebration: The small town with Victorian-style homes and beautifully manicured lawns might remind you a little of **Main Street, U.S.A.**, in the Magic Kingdom. That could be because the residential community was created by Disney, with all the Disney attention to detail. The town has several restaurants that offer great views of a lovely lake. There's also an interactive fountain in the small park near the lake, which is a great spot for the little ones to splash around. To get here take I-4 to Exit 64A and follow the "Celebration" signs.

International Drive: A number of entertainment options, shopping venues, and restaurants are scattered among the hotels that line International Drive. To get to the area, take I-4 Exit 72 or 74A.

Sand Lake Road: This is the part of the city that's nearest the main Disney tourism area, about five minutes or so northeast of International Drive or Universal Orlando. This is an area of Orlando where you'll find some of the city's more upscale stores and restaurants. Over the past few years, **"Restaurant Row"** has sprung up along Sand Lake Road, about a mile west of International Drive. To get to that area, take I-4 Exit 74A.

Central Orlando: Quiet streets lined with huge oak trees can be found all throughout this area. Museums and galleries are situated along main thoroughfares and dozens of **small lakes dot the area**. There are plenty of eateries here but it's also about 30 minutes from the Disney area.

Winter Park: Winter Park is a lovely suburb on the northern end of Orlando, about 25 minutes from Disney. **Dexter's** and some other good restaurants are located here. To get to the area, follow I-4 to Exit 87.

GREAT EATS

From pizza and pasta to sushi, steak and seafood, Central Florida offers unique ambiance and a broad range of menus - something to suit every palate and pocketbook. For special occasions, an elegant evening out, or a vacation meal with the kids in tow, Orlando has what you're looking for. **Ethnic cuisine** is a specialty of Orlando including Chinese, Japanese, Thai, German, Indian, Italian, Cuban and Mexican. Make sure you get a taste of the real Florida while you're here – try gator tail or gator "nuggets" as well as a sampling of Florida's world-famous citrus and Key lime pie.

NIGHTLIFE & ENTERTAINMENT

If you're a night owl, you'll love Orlando when the sun goes down because that's when the city really heats up. From swing or country music to jazz or rock, you'll find something to suit your tastes at entertainment complexes and night spots throughout the city.

SHOPPING

From outlet centers, superstores and flea markets that offer bargains galore and upscale boutiques with one-of-a-kind merchandise lining oak-dotted streets to themed shopping villages and malls which mix retail shops with dining and entertainment, it's a sure bet you'll find something to bring home from your trip.

3. Great One-Day Plans

HIGHLIGHTS

- **The Best of Disney & Orlando**
- **Getting All Wet at Universal**
- **Blast Off to Kennedy Space Center & Seaworld**

INTRO

We've come up with several terrific one-day plans to help you experience the best of Orlando, no matter how long you plan to be here. Whatever brings you to the City Beautiful, spending one day here will only leave you wanting lots more. These quick itineraries focus on plenty of fun and sightseeing, providing something for all ages.

COORDINATES

The major approach routes to **Orlando** are I-95 to westbound I-4 from the Daytona area and the east coast, eastbound I-4 from the Gulf Coast, and I-75 to Florida's Turnpike from the panhandle and beyond. Once in Orlando, the main arterial in the city is **I-4**.

THE BEST OF DISNEY & ORLANDO

Head to **Epcot** and let the fun begin. Grab a **Fastpass** (see sidebar at right) for **Test Track**, one of the most popular rides at Epcot. This ride puts you in a simulator that moves on tracks at high speed. Basically, you're the passenger in a six-seater prototype sports car being tested prior to going into production. The ride puts you through brake tests, sharp turns, near crashes, hill climbs, and paint spraying bays. Pretty cool, right? But the outside lap of the ride gets even more thrilling when the vehicle exceeds 66 mph on a raised roadway around the exterior of the Test Track building. The adrenaline rush is worth the wait.

FASTPASS

Cut down line wait times by using **Fastpass**, Disney's free ride reservation system. Slide your park admission ticket into a turnstile and get an "appointment time" to return to the ride. Fastpass turnstiles are located at the entrances to designated attractions.

Next, check out **Mission: SPACE**, where you can blast off on a simulated ride to Mars - if you can handle the turbulence. This ride isn't for everyone, especially those who get motion sickness. But if you like thrill rides and don't have a problem with things like intense spinning, you'll get a real kick out of the sensation of life-off on this ride. Before you board the four-person rocket capsule, you're assigned to a position: commander, navigator, pilot, or engineer. Passengers can feel the capsule tilt skyward, then it's launch time, which can be quite turbulent but exhilarating. It took about five years for Disney Imagineers, along with the help of 25 experts from NASA to design Mission: SPACE.

After the rides, wander around **World Showcase**, where you can imagine that you're traveling around the world. Learn about Japan, Morocco, Norway, France, Germany and other countries at this spot, which highlights the culture, attractions and cuisine of 11 countries. Located next to a huge man-made lagoon, World Showcase is vast, so you can expect to do a lot of walking. Step into "Mexico" and go on the **Gran Fiesta Tour Starring the Three Caballeros**, an 8 1/2-minute multimedia boat ride that showcases the Maya, Toltec and Aztec civilizations. Visit "Norway" and sail the fjords of Viking explorers. Wander into "France" to see the French countryside and view a replica of the Eiffel Tower. In the afternoon, take the monorail to the Magic Kingdom and jump aboard the steam train at **Main Street, USA**, which takes about 20 minutes to navigate the perimeter of the park. Disembark at **Fantasyland** for child-friendly attractions like "It's a Small World" or at **Frontierland** for older children, where they can enjoy **Big Thunder Mountain Railroad** and **Splash Mountain**. If you get hungry, grab a sandwich or salad at **Pecos Bill's**.

Afterward, make your way to Adventureland and visit **Pirates of the Caribbean**, one of the park's best original rides. Board a small boat and set sail for a 10-minute cruise, taking in a series of scenes depicting a pirate raid on a Caribbean island town. Keep an eye out for Captain Jack Sparrow, Captain Barbossa, sing-

ing marauders, and wily wenches. Then, take a leisurely ride on the **Jungle Cruise**. On your excursion, you'll see plenty of zebras, giraffes, lions, headhunters, and elephants but they're all of the animatronic type. It's a slow-moving attraction, which gives you a chance to catch your breath and relax a bit.

There's a terrific late-afternoon parade over on **Main Street**, so head back that way when you're done with the attractions.

WET 'N' WILD & UNIVERSAL STUDIOS

This next great day starts at **Wet 'n' Wild water park**, reportedly the world's very first water park when it opened in 1977. There are tons of attractions for young children as well as for older thrill-seekers. Spend the day getting all wet and going on exciting rides, tubing adventures, and heart-stopping waterslides. There's a complete water playground for kids, plenty of high-energy slides for adults, a lazy river ride, and even some sandy beaches for working on your tan.

One of the more popular attractions here is **Black Hole**, a two-person tube ride that starts in the light of day and plunges down a pitch-black tube illuminated only by a guiding, glowing line. It's a blast!

Another favorite is **Blue Niagara**, a giant, six-story slide in which twin tubes wrap around each other. Inside is a rushing waterfall. Basically, you are shot through the tubes. A little scary but a heck of a lot of fun.

Lazy River makes for a nice change of pace and slows things down a bit. Settle into an inner tube for a peaceful trip down a gently moving stream. Enjoy basking in the sun as you drift along, just enjoying the day.

When you're ready for some lunch, grab a bite at one of the many concessions in the area where you can get a burger, sandwich, snacks, etc. You can also picnic in the park and coolers are allowed.

Note: the park is scheduled to close down at the end of 2016!

However, glass containers and alcoholic beverages are not permitted. There are many picnic areas scattered around Wet 'n Wild, in both covered and uncovered areas.

Next, **Universal Studios Florida** is a great choice for a few hours of fun. Divided into six "neighborhoods," which wrap themselves around a large lagoon, this park has 444 acres of stage sets, reproductions of New York and San Francisco, shops, moviemaking paraphernalia, and more. The neighborhoods are Production Central; New York; the bicoastal San Francisco/Amity; World Expo; Woody Woodpecker's KidZone; and Hollywood. There are lots of attractions, shows, eateries, and more.

After you're done at the park, make a transition to an evening of winding down at **Universal CityWalk**, a huge entertainment complex offering a broad range of restaurants and nightclubs to satisfy most tastes. Favorite dining spots include Jimmy Buffet's Margaritaville, Emeril's Restaurant Orlando, and the Hard Rock Cafe. Well into the evening, DJ's play the latest in hip-hop, jazz-fusion and techno at the Groove, one of CityWalk's happening clubs. At CityJazz, the two-story club pays homage to jazz with music and its more than 500 pieces of memorabilia representing Dixieland, swing, bebop and modern jazz.

KENNEDY CENTER & SEAWORLD

Today, it's time to blast off - to Florida's beautiful Space Coast, about 45 minutes east of Orlando, on NASA Parkway SR 405. Spend the early part of the day at **Kennedy Space Center Visitor Complex**. If you're ready for a genuine Space Age experience, then it's all systems go at this exciting spot - the launch and landing site for the space shuttle. Take a tour of space shuttle launch facilities, meet an astronaut, and see the collection of eight authentic rockets from past eras. You've always wanted to touch a chunk of Mars? Well, you can do that here, too.

There are lots of exhibits and other attractions to take in, including the Astronaut Memorial, a tribute to those who have died while in pursuit of space exploration. You can grab a snack or light lunch here too. You should be aware that roads within the space center are closed to the public, and all visits start at the visitor complex. From there, buses take you on tours throughout the facility. *Info: 407/449-4444.*

Next up is **SeaWorld Orlando**, where you can marvel at the beauty of killer whales at The Shamu Adventure; enjoy the replicas of Caribbean habitats at Key West at SeaWorld; and partake of the popular Manatee Rescue show. People always associate SeaWorld with Shamu and that's cool but there's a lot more to this attraction than Shamu. Every single attraction at the park is designed to showcase the beauty of the marine world and show ways that we can protect its waters and wildlife.

There are only a handful of rides in the park but that doesn't mean you won't have plenty of fun. SeaWorld's performance venues, activities, and attractions surround a 17-acre lake but you'll soon realize that the park is set up in such a way that it's a natural progression from one show or attraction to the next. It's an easy park to navigate.

One of our favorite attractions (yes, we like to chase adventure) is **Kraken**. At 149 feet it's the second-tallest roller coaster in Florida. With seven inversions, moments of weightlessness, and floorless seats, it's one serious (and fun) coaster! You might have to wait in line for this one but it's worth the wait.

Another favorite is the P**enguin Encounter**. Don't you just love the overly-adorable penguins? About 17 species of penguin are waddling around a refrigerated re-creation of Antarctica at this attraction. To keep them cool, they are showered with three tons of snow each day. Nearby, you can also enjoy a viewing area of puffins and murres.

You won't want to miss Shamu Stadium where the guest of honor is **Shamu**, SeaWorld's orca mascot. In the show he puts on, Shamu and other whales perform beautifully choreographed moves against the backdrop of an elaborate three-story set. Don't forget that these whales weigh up to 10,000 pounds each, so their grace and agility as they perform is awe-inspiring to watch.

After a long day, wrap things up with a relaxing dinner at SeaWorld. Try the **Sharks Underwater Grill**, a comfortable but somewhat upscale restaurant. Five bay windows separate the dining room from a gigantic aquarium filled with Atlantic black tip sharks, tiger, sandbar, black nose, and others. Menu choices include Caribbean-spice seafood pasta, filet mignon with jerk seasoning, and pork medallions with black-bean sauce.

4. The Best of Walt Disney World

HIGHLIGHTS

- Magic Kingdom
- EPCOT
- Hollywood Studios
- Animal Kingdom
- Disney Water Parks
- Disney Springs

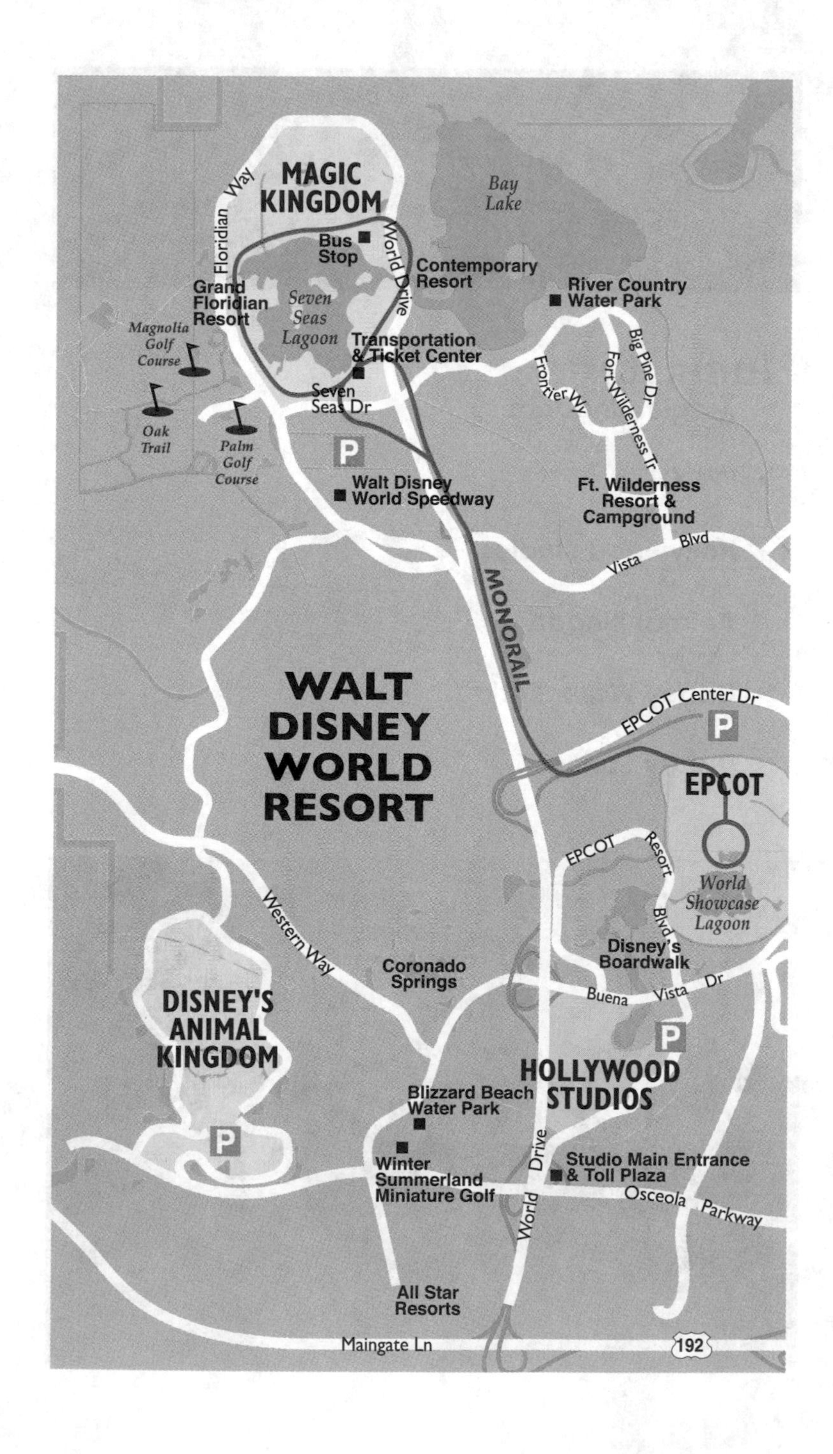
MAGIC KINGDOM
Bay Lake
Floridian Way
Bus Stop
World Drive
Contemporary Resort
River Country Water Park
Grand Floridian Resort
Seven Seas Lagoon
Magnolia Golf Course
Transportation & Ticket Center
Big Pine Dr
Frontier Wy
Fort Wilderness Tr
Seven Seas Dr
Oak Trail
Palm Golf Course
P
Walt Disney World Speedway
Ft. Wilderness Resort & Campground
Vista Blvd
MONORAIL
WALT DISNEY WORLD RESORT
EPCOT Center Dr
P
EPCOT
EPCOT Resort Blvd
World Showcase Lagoon
Western Way
Disney's Boardwalk
Coronado Springs
Buena Vista Dr
DISNEY'S ANIMAL KINGDOM
P
HOLLYWOOD STUDIOS
Blizzard Beach Water Park
P
Winter Summerland Miniature Golf
World Drive
Studio Main Entrance & Toll Plaza
Osceola Parkway
All Star Resorts
Maingate Ln
192

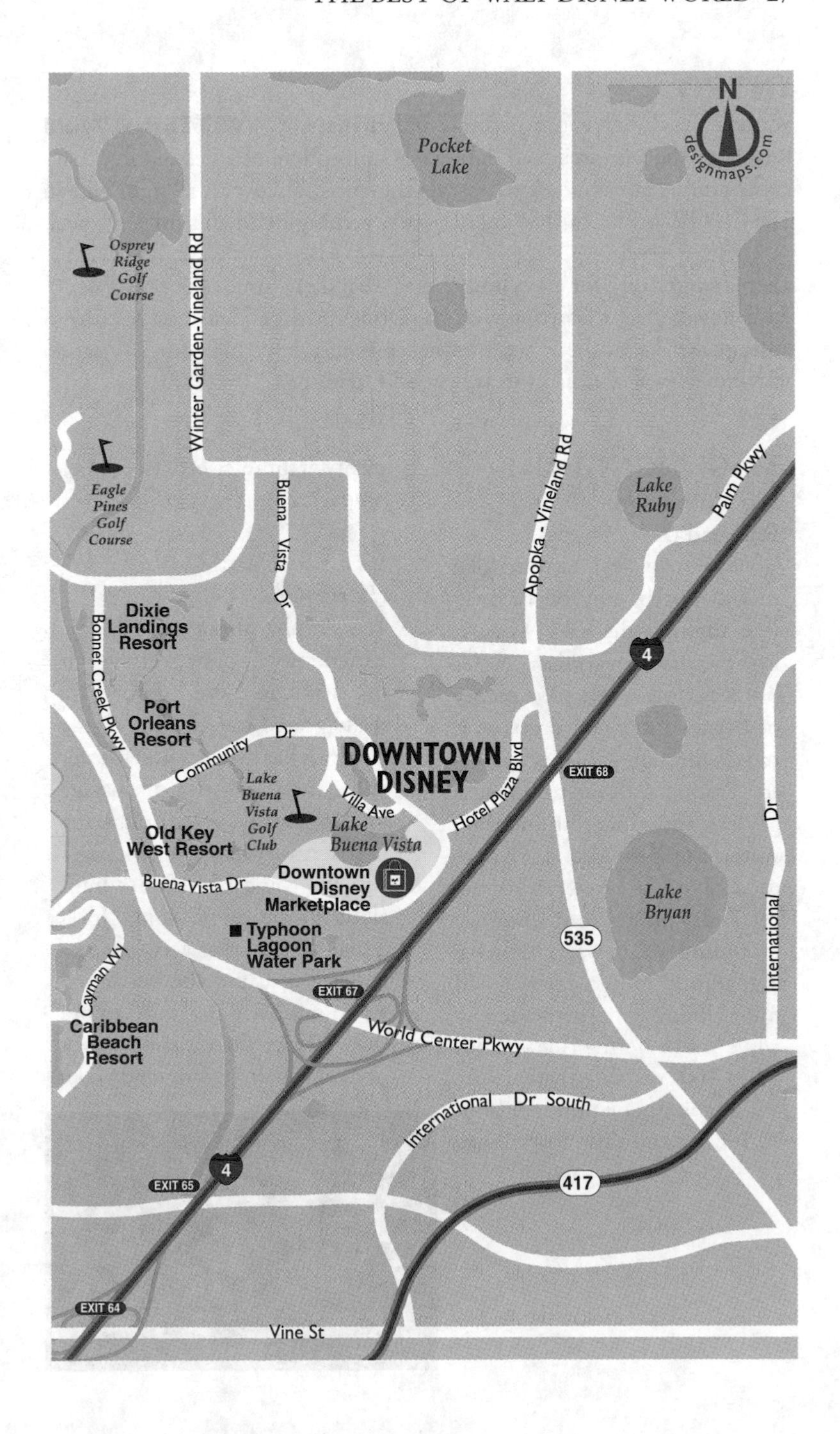
designmaps.com
N
Pocket Lake
Osprey Ridge Golf Course
Winter Garden-Vineland Rd
Eagle Pines Golf Course
Buena Vista Dr
Apopka - Vineland Rd
Lake Ruby
Palm Pkwy
Dixie Landings Resort
Bonnet Creek Pkwy
Port Orleans Resort
Community Dr
DOWNTOWN DISNEY
Hotel Plaza Blvd
Lake Buena Vista Golf Club
Villa Ave
Lake Buena Vista
Old Key West Resort
Buena Vista Dr
Downtown Disney Marketplace
Typhoon Lagoon Water Park
4
EXIT 68
International Dr
Lake Bryan
535
Cayman Wy
EXIT 67
Caribbean Beach Resort
World Center Pkwy
International Dr South
417
EXIT 65
EXIT 64
Vine St

INTRO

Whether it's the adventure, wonder and excitement of **Walt Disney World Resort** or the sun-drenched, laid-back atmosphere of a destination that's known for its fine dining and upscale shopping, discover it all right here in The City Beautiful. In this chapter, we're zeroing in on all things Disney!

There's **something for everybody** here. We'll share some of our favorites in the following pages, starting with the Disney parks and attractions within those parks. From there, we'll branch out and delve into other Orlando activities as well as nearby areas beyond Orlando.

MAGIC KINGDOM

Big Thunder Mountain Railroad (*Frontierland*)

Board a runaway mine train for a meandering, bumpy roller coaster ride through the Old West. It isn't the fastest or wildest coaster but this classic does have plenty of twists, turns, and drops as it travels through gold-rush country. Passing in front of spewing geysers and under thundering waterfalls provides a chance to cool off as you rattle past 20 audio-animatronic figures, including donkeys, chickens, a goat, and even a grizzled old miner. Enjoy taking in the scenery while you're on the ride - about $300,000 worth of authentic antique mining equipment, hot springs, a mining town, and plenty of tumbleweeds (see photo on page 25).

It's a Small World (*Fantasyland*)

You simply cannot go to Magic Kingdom without checking out this attraction, even though it's really geared to kids. The classic boat ride has been around forever and is almost a rite of passage for those who come through the park's gates. No matter what age you are, you can't help but hum along to the catchy song "It's a Small World" that accompanies the ride because the costumed audio-animatronic dolls (more than 425 of them!) sing it over and over again in munchkin-like

voices. The dolls are everything from Indian snake charmers and Chinese acrobats to Swiss yodelers and Spanish flamenco dancers. We're still humming.

STOP ELBOWING ME!

If you have babies, small children, or senior citizens in your group, you may want to avoid visiting the Disney parks in the summer because it can be very difficult to navigate your way through the crowds. Additionally, any holiday when the kids are out of school (Presidents' Day weekend for example), will bring huge crowds to the Disney parks.

Jungle Cruise
(*Adventureland*)
This ride takes you on a 10-minute tour of four "continents" and four rivers, the **Congo**, the **Nile**, the **Mekong**, and the **Amazon**. Your boats have whimsical names like Amazon Annie and the tour guides are full of info, tips, and corny jokes. As your guide navigates through the water, keep an eye on the shore for rhinos, zebras, lions, and elephants (albeit animatronic ones) You'll also go right under a waterfall, a welcome diversion on a hot day.

Pirates Of The Caribbean
(*Adventureland*)
Ahoy, mates! Travel through a pseudo Caribbean town as fierce-looking pirates are looting and plundering all around you. As you board the boats, a ghostly voice can be heard saying, "Dead men tell no tales." It's all in good fun, even if it's not entirely politically correct (rowdy pirates chase after saucy wenches while swigging bottles of rum.) Hundreds of audio-animatronic figures, including pigs, chickens, dogs, cats, and donkeys, populate the town, adding realism.

Space Mountain
(*Tomorrowland*)
Grab a seat on this exciting roller coaster, still the most popular

thrill ride in the park, and blast off into space. The hairpin turns and cosmic effects of this **180-foot-high attraction**, along with being in the dark, make it a thrilling ride. The plunges, twists, and turns on this indoor coaster make it seem like you're traveling at a pretty high rate of speed but you're moving at a relatively tame 28 mph.

Splash Mountain
(*Frontierland*)
There's a kiosk near this log-flume water ride (see photo at right) that sells lapel pins, caps and T-shirts with the message "Splash Mountain - Dry Is Not An Option." Believe the hype. Though the journey starts off as a smooth glide through calm water, delicious anticipation soon sets in as the vessel climbs up a steep hill, teeters at the top, and then **careens downhill as a wall of water washes over you**. Even though we got drenched from head to toe, and had water sloshing out of our tennis shoes, we promptly got back in line for another ride. You're almost guaranteed to get wet no matter where you sit but if you want to get a really good soaking ask the ride attendant if you can sit in the front row.

Stitch's Great Escape
(*Tomorrowland*)
The little ones will especially enjoy this new attraction that's based on the movie, *Lilo & Stitch*. Centered around a back-story to the film, about the mischievous Stitch before he meets Lilo in Hawaii, it's full of antics and sensory effects. You might like to know that Stitch is the first audio-animatronic figure that spits!

The Haunted Mansion

(Liberty Square)

More fun than scary, this ride is a longtime favorite. Climb into your Doom Buggy and take a deep breath as you zoom past such **eerie scenes** as a graveyard band, chandeliers draped in cobwebs, a talking head in a crystal ball, and flying objects. Scary music and non-stop howling complete the realistic ambience. And a "ghost" joins you in the Doom Buggy at the end.

SO DEMAGNETIZING

Theme park tickets can demagnetize easily so you might want to keep them somewhere separately from your credit cards. If your ticket won't swipe at the park turnstiles, Disney will replace it but it involves making a trip to Guest Relations and that can be a bummer, especially if it happens just when you're ready to board a ride.

EPCOT

Mission: SPACE

(Future World)

You don't want to miss this white-knuckle thrill ride, a

simulated space adventure. (Well, unless you have problems with motion sickness.) If not, **buckle up and get ready for launch**. You can choose to be pilot, navigator, engineer or commander on your mission to "Mars." Then, it's time for blast off! As you get a small taste of what it's like to be an astronaut, you'll experience a pulse-racing liftoff, intense spinning, and weightlessness in the deep reach of "outer space" before you come back to earth.

Soarin'

(The Land)

If you're afraid of heights, sit this one out. Otherwise, you'll have a blast on this high-flying new attraction. Enjoy the breeze as you "fly" along California's awesome landscapes. The ride uses motion-based technology to lift you in your seat about 40 feet into the air within a giant projection-screen dome. So cool! You'll soar above the Golden Gate Bridge, Yosemite, Napa Valley, and other California attractions. Besides feeling the rush of wind, you'll enjoy the scents of pine forests and orange blossoms.

Test Track
(*Future World*)
If putting a test car through its paces sounds fun, this exciting, mile-long attraction is right up your alley. With plenty of sharp curves, brake tests, a tire-squealing hill climb, and exhilarating take-offs and stops, you're in for a real **adrenaline rush**. Our favorite part was the tail end of this thrilling ride – a 12-second, 65-mph burst of speed that left us breathless and wanting more.

World Showcase Pavilions
(*World Showcase*)
Want to travel to exotic places like Japan (see photo below), Morocco, Norway, France, Germany, and other countries? You can do that (sort of) at the World Showcase Pavilions, which highlights the culture, attractions, and cuisine of **11 different countries**. For instance, step into "Mexico" and go on the El Rio del Tiempo, an eight-minute multimedia boat ride that showcases the Yucatan's Mayan pyramids. Visit "Norway" and sail the fjords of viking explorers. Wander into "France" and learn about the French countryside, and view a replica of the Eiffel Tower.

MEETING PRINCESSES
If you can't get reservations for the princess character meal at Cinderella Castle and don't want to disappoint the little girl in your life, you might consider trying to line up a reservation for the princess meal in the **Norway Pavilion of Epcot**. It's not quite as popular but still fun.

HOLLYWOOD STUDIOS

Rock 'n' Roller Coaster
Feel the need for speed? This coaster delivers. You'll shake, rattle, and roll as your 24-passenger "car" flies along the tracks. There are multiple inversions as it zooms from 0 to 60 mph in a matter of 2.8 seconds. It's a blast. But as you step off the ride, you may feel like you've been at a rock concert because each car has 120 speakers that blare Aerosmith tunes at full volume. Sorry, ear plugs aren't provided!

Toy Story Mania!
This popular new interactive adventure involves an interactive "Toy Story" competition inspired by the film. 3-D glasses put you in the middle of the action as you board vehicles and zip into a world of exciting midway-style games hosted by your favorite characters. It may sound a little strange but it's way cool.

Twilight Zone Tower of Terror
If you enjoy the feeling of being really scared but having fun at the same time, this ride is for you. Walk past faded signs and dead shrubbery (it's all part of the attraction), and continue on as corridors lead to a dark library. You can hear a storm raging outside and there are eerie

sounds and creaking noises inside, too. The **dramatic finale** arrives when you board your elevator - a 13-story free fall, with passengers screaming all the way down (and then it quickly shoots back up and down several times before the ride ends.) Yep, we screamed too. And immediately got back in line for another turn.

ANIMAL KINGDOM

Expedition Everest

(*Asia*)

Hop aboard this high-speed, coaster-like train and get your thrills as it moves forward and backward through glaciers, bamboo forests, **waterfalls and canyons** as you go higher and higher through snowcapped mountain peaks. At ride's end, a yeti appears and the vehicle plunges backward briefly.

Kali River Rapids

(*Asia*)

You'll have a blast on your white-water rafting adventure down the churning waters of the "Chakranadi River" (see photo below). Traveling on your 12-person circular raft through jungle mists and past spewing geysers, **you'll definitely get wet but that's the whole idea**. It's a rather tame ride, although there is one exciting drop down the roaring rapids.

Kilimanjaro Safaris

(*Africa*)

Join the hunt for "poachers" and Little Red, a missing baby elephant, as your jeep-like vehicle takes you on an **adventurous safari** across a rolling savannah. You're in for a real treat as you get the chance to glimpse elephants, giraffes, lions, rhinos, wallabies,

zebras, and gazelles. Sometimes, animals run right alongside the jeep. At the end of the ride, everyone delights in the excitement when poachers are foiled and Little Red turns up safe and sound.

The Boneyard
(DinoLand U.S.A.)
A **prehistoric playground** that's built around replicas of the fossil remains of Triceratops, T-Rex, and other dinosaurs, this favorite area for kids (and kids at heart), is both educational and fun. So, go ahead and slide, crawl, and slither until you're worn out. Explorers can even dig up the "bones" of a wooly mammoth.

DISNEY WATER PARKS

Blizzard Beach
It's about the chills and thrills (and getting all wet!) at this super-fun park with pools, water slides and waterfalls. At Summit Plummet, get your adrenaline racing on what's billed as the tallest and fastest water slide in the United States. If a 55-mph plunge sounds too exciting, grab a tube and take a leisurely trip down Cross Country Creek. Then, check out **Snow Stormers**, where you can take a 350-ft-long flume ride from Mount Gushmore down through a backcountry course complete with ski-style slalom gates. The little ones might enjoy Tike's Peak, a kid-sized version of Blizzard Beach, which has racer slides, tube slides, and a splash fountain.

ACCIDENTALLY TOPLESS

Oops! Girls and women might want to consider wearing one-piece swimsuits at the water parks. According to cast members who work at the parks, several women a day end up losing their swimsuit tops during adventure rides, especially during descents into the water.

Typhoon Lagoon

The surf's always up at this tropical playground that's a paradise for snorkeling, sliding and body-surfing. At **Shark Reef**, enjoy a saltwater snorkeling adventure around a sunken tanker with sharks and schools of multi-colored tropical fish. There are **several falls** here – Mayday, Gang Plank and Keelhaul – where you can raft down rapids, race through rock formations, and careen through caves. Spend some time in the Surf Pool and catch some 6-foot waves in a lagoon that's bigger than two football fields! The kiddos might get a kick out of **Ketchakiddie Creek**, where they can choose from 20 different water activities, including slides and floating boats.

DISNEY SPRINGS

Marketplace

Shop 'til you drop at **the largest World of Disney store** in the country. Browse for T-shirts of your favorite characters, as well as any Disney-related memorabilia (watches, caps, stuffed animals, pins, jewelry, etc.) you could possibly imagine. Or look for the perfect toy or game at **Once Upon a Toy**, a toy-lover's dream store come true. Check out games such as Princess Monopoly or the Pirates of the

of the Caribbean Game of Life. At the **LEGO Imagination Center**, you can build whatever your heart desires.

When you're ready for lunch or dinner, **Fulton's Crab House** is a fine choice. Set in a replica of an old riverboat, with a dining room decorated in a nautical theme, the eatery is a traditional seafood house. For entrees, choose from fresh fish and crab to prime cuts of succulent filet mignon and juicy roasted chicken.

The Landing
Formerly known as Pleasure Island, this used to be where locals and tourists alike headed to dance the night away but this area has been undergoing a transformation and the dance clubs have been done away with. Still, there is plenty to see and do here! At **Raglan Road**, which resembles an authentic Irish pub, enjoy entertainment, food, and grab a pint. Live entertainment gets going about 9 p.m. each evening.

For more dining options, check out **Paradiso 37**, an eatery overlooking Village Lake. The menu offers up North, Central, and South American cuisine. Try the tapas plate or a sausage and pepper hoagie. The Argentinean skirt steak with grilled barbecue shrimp is a real stand-out. How about decadent Chilean sopapillas for dessert? There's also an international wine and tequila bar.

The **Food Trucks Exposition Park** located in Disney Springs is a new attraction. Food trucks, gaining popularity in other parts of the country too, are a hit because they offer up so many options. The trucks here serve a variety of items, from tandoori spice shrimp to sweet potato puffs topped with marshmallow cream to buffalo-style chicken served with cornbread waffles, and everything in between.

West Side
This is where you'll find more restaurants, shops, and a 24-screen movie theater. A favorite eatery

is **Bongo's Cuban Cafe**, created by singer Gloria Estefan and her husband, Emilio. The interior, with vivid hand-painted murals, and palm fronds, is intended to remind visitors of a 1950s-era Cuba. Try the Filete de Pescado a la Catalana, lightly floured filet of fish with creole sauce. Or consider **Wolfgang Puck Cafe** for dinner and dig in to pizza or sushi.

After dinner, take in one of the hottest shows in town, **La Nouba** at **Cirque du Soleil**. The exciting production, a blend of circus art and theatrics, features exotic costumes, acrobatics, original sets, and unforgettable music. On Sundays, head to the **House of Blues** for live gospel music and a Southern-style all-you-can-eat buffet.

Get your shopping fix here too. **Suspended Animation** has Disney posters, cels, prints, and more. At the shop **Curl by Sammy Duval**, a high end surf shop, you can browse for surf boards, clothing, and accessories. Check out **DisneyQuest Emporium** for clothes and other merchandise. At **Pop Gallery**, browse for high-end gift items including sculptures and paintings. Stroll in to **D Street** and you'll find pop culture novelties and apparel. **Disney's Candy Cauldron** is perfect for your sweet tooth with an abundance of sweets to choose from. Get your fill of hard candy, chocolate, fudge, and other decadent offerings.

5. Disney's Best Sleeps & Eats

HIGHLIGHTS

All of the Disney hotels operate under the family plan, which means that kids 18 and under stay free with parents. When you check in, you'll be issued a resort ID that allows you to charge meals, drinks, tickets, and souvenirs to your room and also gives you access to all Disney World transportation. Why stay at a Disney property? Convenience, convenience, convenience! For starters, staying on-site allows you unlimited use of the monorails, buses, and boats of the Disney transportation system.

As for dining at Walt Disney World, your options are endless. Your only dilemma will be deciding where to eat because there are a huge number as well as variety of eateries here. In this chapter we list restaurants throughout the park, as well as a separate section beginning on page 56 listing the best eats in each hotel.

In this chapte, hotels are highlighted in **red**, restaurants in **purple**.

BEST SLEEPS & EATS

MAGIC KINGDOM SLEEPS

Contemporary Resort $$$$

If you like busy hotels where there seems to be a constant buzz of activity, you'll probably like this resort. There are more than one thousand hotel rooms and the lobby is chock full of shops and restaurants. It's on the monorail line and is one of the easiest Magic Kingdom resorts to book. If you're into sports, you'll be happy with the choices of tennis, parasailing and waterskiing. Check out Chef Mickey's restaurant for breakfast or dinner and you're almost guaranteed to meet some favorite Disney characters. *Info: 407/824-1000.*

Fort Wilderness Resort & Campground $

You'll find campsites for tents and RVS here as well as air-conditioned cabins. The cabins sleep six and rent for around the same nightly rate as a luxury hotel but if you're looking for a bargain, you can't beat the tent sites and hookups for lodging options - unless camping isn't your idea of a vacation. With its spacious surroundings, the campground is ideal for families and perfect for outdoor excursions like biking and volleyball. Fort Wilderness also has a variety of activities for kids, including horseback riding and hayrides. Many visitors enjoy the convenience of shopping for groceries at the on-site trading post. *Info: 407/824-2900.*

HOTEL PRICE KEY

$	starting below $100
$$	starting at $100-$150
$$$	starting at $150-$200
$$$$	starting above $200

Grand Floridian Resort & Spa $$$$

With its gabled roofs, white verandas, and high ceilings (see photo on previous page), this is one of the prettiest properties within Disney. There are several programs for children, including the Wonderland

Tea Party, Disney's Pirate Adventures, and Grand Adventures in Cooking. An on-site health club and full-service spa are appealing. *Info: 407/824-3000.*

The Polynesian Resort $$$$
Guests stay in one of the lovely and sprawling "houses" along the lagoon. From The Polynesian, you'll have access to monorail, ferry, and launch service. There's also a private beach with a nice pool, plus several boating options. An on-site child-care center is a real plus. And make sure to check out the Kona Cafe, popular for its luscious desserts. *Info: 407/824-2000.*

Wilderness Lodge & Villas $$$$
You can't miss the Western theme of this hotel because it seeps into every corner of the property. And it's why many families return over and over again. The hotel's 82-foot fireplace burns year round. Children ride stick ponies to their tables in the Whispering Canyon Cafe. And the staff here dress in attire similar to what park rangers wear. Kids of all ages never seem to tire of the pool area and its erupting geyser. But do note that this is the only Magic Kingdom resort without monorail service. *Info: 407/824-3200.*

DINING PRICE KEY

$	under $25 per person
$$	$25-50 per person
$$$	$50-100 per person
$$$$	over $100 per person

MAGIC KINGDOM EATS

Casey's Corner (Main Street) $

This casual baseball-themed eatery has all of your favorite ballpark foods: jumbo hot dogs, chili dogs, corn dogs, and French fries. Grab one of the charming round tables outside and watch the world go by.

Cinderella's Royal Table (Fantasyland) $$$

You don't have to be Cinderella to eat at Cinderella's Royal Table in Cinderella Castle. But you can still be treated like royalty

(servers call everyone "Lord" or "Lady.) Entrees include prime rib, spice-crusted salmon, New York strip, and roasted chicken. Cinderella appears at various times during the day to greet visitors. When you make your reservation, ask what times she is scheduled to appear. This is also home to the very popular "Once Upon a Time" princess character breakfasts and the "A Fairy Tale" lunches. Try to book your character meal at least 6 months in advance (seriously!) or you might miss out on the experience. Reservations required.

Columbia Harbour House (Liberty Square) $

A cozy fast-food fish house that's filled with antiques, model ships, and nautical instruments, you can enjoy a good meal here. Choose from fried fish, vegetarian chili, clam chowder, fried chicken strips, salads, or sandwiches.

Cosmic Ray's Starlight Cafe (Tomorrowland) $

The fast-food joint is the largest counter serve restaurant in the Magic Kingdom. Choose from sandwiches, salads, vegetarian burgers, and wraps as well as the usual hamburgers and chicken fingers. Best of all, the line moves fast and there's plenty of seating. Nobody said it was gourmet but it works well in a pinch, especially if everyone in your group is hungry and tired.

Crystal Palace (Main Street) $

Kids (and kids at heart) will love the fact that Winnie the Pooh and friends circulate among diners. The buffet is pretty good and there's plenty of choices, including lots of vegetables, chicken, pastas, fish, and carved meats. There's even an ice-cream sundae bar where you can make your own concoction. Reservations are necessary unless you plan to dine at an off time, such as 4 p.m.

Liberty Tree Tavern (Liberty Square) $

For lunch, enjoy salads, sandwiches, pot roast, and New England clam chowder at this restaurant that resembles the style of colonial Williamsburg. Dinner is an all-you-can-eat Thanksgiving-style feast that includes turkey and stuffing, macaroni and cheese, flank steak, and many other favorites. Disney characters, dressed in Revolutionary War-era costumes, visit with guests during dinner.

Pecos Bill Cafe (Frontierland) $

One of the most popular fast-food restaurants in the Magic Kingdom, this is a hit with adults and kids alike because of its comfortable surroundings, large portions, and variety of meal choices. We return to this one again and again. You'll find everything from hamburgers and hot dogs to salads and chicken wrap sandwiches. Eat indoors or head to a table outside.

Pinocchio Village Haus (Fantasyland) $

This cozy eatery has several rooms for dining and is decorated with antiques and murals of characters from Pinocchio's story. See if you can spot Cleo the Goldfish or Figaro the Cat. Fare includes Italian sandwiches, pizza, soups, and salads. Some of the tables next to windows overlook the "It's a Small World" attraction.

Tony's Town Square (Main Street) $$

For lunch, choices are sandwiches, pizza, salads, or pasta. At dinner, favorites include chicken Florentine or grilled pork chop. While deciding which Italian sweets to order for dessert, enjoy the decor, inspired by Walt Disney's classic, *Lady and the Tramp*. Reservations suggested.

EPCOT SLEEPS

BoardWalk Inn & Villas $$$$

We like this one a lot and if you like being somewhere where there's always a buzz of activity, it will be one of your favorites too. The BoardWalk Inn & Villas are the hub of a complex that houses the ESPN sports club, several restaurants and shops, a piano bar, and a dance club. There's something going on along the waterfront until late in the evening every night, so things are hopping here. It's also super close to both Epcot and Hollywood Studios as well as a reasonable distance from the Magic Kingdom and Animal Kingdom. You'll find lots of entertainment options, including midway games, surrey bikes for rent, plenty of restaurants and bars, on-site child-care facilities, and a health club. *Info: 407/939-5100.*

Caribbean Beach $$$$

Set on 200 acres southeast of Epcot and near Disney's Hollywood Studios, Caribbean Beach is comprised of five vibrantly colored villages of sorts surrounding a 45-acre lake called Barefoot Bay. There are more than 2,000 rooms, making the property one of the largest hotels in the United States. The decor, furnishings, and apparel of staff, all reflect a Caribbean theme and each "village" fits a different Caribbean island - Aruba, Barbados, Jamaica, Martinique, and Trinidad. There's a food court, restaurant and lounge, arcade, and shops as well as a recreation area that features a pool with waterfalls

and a slide; a beach; and an area where boats and bicycles can be rented. *Info: 407/934-3400.*

Yacht & Beach Club and Beach Club Villas $$$$

Conjure up images of the New England seaside and you'll know what to expect when visiting this property. A lighthouse on the pier welcomes guests and a nautical theme is used throughout the resort as well as in the rooms. When it comes to activities and entertainment, you'll find enough here to take up your entire vacation if that's what you choose. A few options include miniature golf, boating, fishing excursions, health club, tennis, an arcade, and more. *Info: 407/934-8000.*

Swan & Dolphin $$$$

These are sister resorts but you can tell them apart easily - just look for the 47-foot-swan and the 56-foot-dolphin and you'll know which property is which. The lovely surroundings include waterfalls and lots of palm trees. Each of the properties has several terrific restaurants as well as lounges. You'll never run out of things to do and can pick from activities such as swimming, boating, golf, spas, shopping, health club, tennis, and much more. There's also a children's program, Camp Dolphin, which welcomes children ages 4-12 and offers supervised activities from 5:30 p.m. to midnight. Cost is $10 per child per hour. *Info: 407/934-3000.*

EPCOT EATS

Biergarten (World Showcase Pavilions) $$

It's Oktoberfest every day here. Enjoy specialties like sauerbraten, chicken schnitzel, sausages, pork, rosemary roast chicken and more. Musicians in lederhosen entertain while you dine and a fun, party atmosphere abounds. The dinner buffet includes more choices and is pricier but the lunch buffet is just as good and less costly.

Coral Reef (Future World) $$

Offering a terrific panoramic view of the coral reef through huge windows, fare includes what you'd expect - fresh fish and shellfish. Choose from shrimp, catfish, salmon, and more, prepared in a variety of ways. You can also order items such as grilled chicken breast or New York strip steak. Reservations suggested.

Garden Grill (Future World) $$$

There's a nightly character dinner here hosted by Chip and Dale and the menu includes fried catfish and rotisserie meats. Lunch is no longer served at this eatery. Reservations suggested.

Electric Umbrella (Future World) $

A fast-food eatery with lots of offerings, choose from burgers, chicken salad, veggie wraps, chicken strips, sandwiches, and more.

Le Cellier Steakhouse (World Showcase Pavilions) $$

One of the most popular restaurants in Epcot, Le Cellier serves up the juiciest and tastiest steaks around. If steak isn't your thing, go for another excellent choice - the salmon. Cheese soup is also a favorite. Save some room for dessert because the restaurant is also known for its delectable sweet creations like the chocolate cake that's one of our favorites.

Rose & Crown Dining Room (World Showcase Pavilions) $$
A charming bar and restaurant, the Rose & Crown features live entertainment, friendly service, and fare such as meat pies and fish-and-chips. Dine outside on the patio and you can enjoy a great view of the World Showcase Lagoon.

Sunshine Seasons (Future World) $
It's fast food but several cuisines are served at various counters, so each family member can get whatever they want and then join everyone at the table. For instance, it has a sandwich area where you can get a variety of sandwiches; a soup and salad section; a grill area featuring rotisserie chicken, beef, grilled salmon and more; and a wok section serving up things like Mongolian beef with jasmine rice, and noodle bowls.

DISNEY'S HOLLYWOOD STUDIOS
ABC Commissary $$
The name alone has that certain star quality that makes you want to check it out. But you're here for some grub and the commissary has plenty of choices at reasonable prices. Selections include cheeseburgers, chicken curry, fish and chips, Cuban sandwiches vegetable noodle stir-fry, and tabbouleh. Kids have their choice of stand-by's like chicken nuggets or macaroni and cheese.

50's Prime Time Cafe $$

Step into this fun, affordable eatery and get your fill of comfort food. The menu features favorites like pot roast, meat loaf, fried chicken, grilled pork chops, and pot pies. Enjoy clips of old TV favorites "I Love Lucy" and "The Honeymooners" while you eat your meal on Formica tables. For something sweet, a malt, milkshake, or sundae is divine. Your waitress, otherwise known as "Mom," stops by

your table often to make sure you're minding your manners and keeping your elbows off the table. You'd think that would get annoying but it's so kitschy it's cute.

Hollywood Brown Derby $$

Caricatures of movie stars line the walls of this slightly formal restaurant, so you may feel as if you've stepped back into Old Hollywood. Dining options include fresh seafood, pasta, veal and a signature Cobb salad.

Rosie's All American Cafe $

This charming, casual eatery with outdoor seating offers up chicken strips, cheeseburgers, veggie burgers, salads, and more. A slice of apple pie is a nice way to finish up lunch.

Sci Fi Dine-In Theatre $

Modeled after old drive-in theatres where you eat in your car. The setting is unique but the fare it serves is the usual burgers, sandwiches, pasta, and salads. A favorite is the reuben sandwich.

Toy Story Pizza Planet $$

This restaurant is fun, has fast service, pretty good pizza and salads, and to top it all off there's an arcade area that will keep the kids happy while waiting for their meal to arrive.

ANIMAL KINGDOM SLEEPS

All-Star Movies, Music & Sports $

As value resorts, these All-Star properties don't offer many frills but the whimsical atmosphere and service makes the resorts big hits, especially with kids. The All-Star Sports is, as you'd imagine, the place for sports fans. Huge, brightly-colored baseball bats, football helmets, surfboards, and other sporting memorabilia adorn the buildings. At the All-Star Music resort, the themes include rock, country, jazz, and calypso. Check out the walk-through, neon-lit jukebox. The All-Star Movie resort celebrates movie classics, including Disney films such as 101 Dalmatians and Toy Story. Buildings are decorated with 40-foot dalmatians and huge versions of Buzz Lightyear and Woody. *Info: All-Star Sports, 407/939-5000; All-Star Music, 407/939-6000; or All-Star Movies, 407/939-7000.*

Coronado Springs $$$$

The resort reveals its Mexican theme in several ways, including Spanish-tile roofs, adobe walls, and a Mayan ruin-themed pool. The rooms are scattered around a lovely 15-acre lake. There's a full-service restaurant as well as a food court. If you want to pursue water sports or other outdoor activities, you're in the right place. Choose from boating, fishing excursions, swimming, bikes and surrey bikes, and more. *Info: 407/939-1000.*

Disney's Animal Kingdom Lodge & Villas $$$$

A wonderful re-creation of an African savanna pretty much surrounds this resort, so don't be surprised when you see (or hear) exotic birds, zebras, giraffes, and more. In fact, you could be standing on your balcony here and be practically eyeball-to-eyeball with a giraffe. The resort is only about a mile from the Animal Kingdom park, so if you plan to spend a lot of time there this would be a convenient place to stay. The lobby is filled with African artwork and artifacts, and a popular place to hang out. This is where you'll find the four-story observation deck where you can enjoy spotting wildlife. *Info: 407/938-3000.*

Pop Century $

Like the All-Star resorts, Pop Century celebrates all things Americana. The 2,880-room resort is devoted to representing the second half of the twentieth century. A cool feature is its larger-than-life time capsules, commemorating the toys, dance crazes, fads, and catchphrases that swept the nation in the time period of 1950s-1990s. Groovy, right? Even the swimming pools are in fun shapes: a computer, flower, and bowling pin. There's a food court with a bakery, market, and food stands offering up burgers, pasta, and pizza. *Info: 407/938-4000.*

ANIMAL KINGDOM EATS

Flame Tree Barbecue (Discovery Island) $

Smoked barbecue ribs, chicken and beef, as well as pork sandwiches, are on the menu at this casual, affordable restaurant that dishes up heaping portions. Our favorite is the tasty pork sandwich, which comes with french fries and baked beans. For lighter choices, go for a fresh fruit salad, or a green salad with barbecue chicken. Kids will likely make a beeline for the peanut butter and jelly sandwiches or beanie weanies.

Pizzafari (Safari Village) $

Enjoy a variety of pizzas, sandwiches, and salads at this laid-back eatery. The chicken parmesan sandwich is a favorite, pizzas are pretty good too.

Rainforest Cafe (at main entrance of park) $$

Located in a recreated tropical jungle with dramatic "thunderstorms" taking place inside the restaurant throughout your meal. Good info to have in case you find that sort of thing annoying. Kids seem to get a kick out of it, though. Waterfalls, fish tanks, and large trees add to to the setting. The menu includes pastas, salads, sandwiches, hamburgers, and more. Of note is that the restaurant is accessible from inside or outside the park, which means admission to the park isn't necessary to enter. Reservations suggested. See photo on next page.

Restaurantosaurus (DinoLand USA) $
Situated in DinoLand U.S.A., the eatery is themed as a campsite of sorts for student paleontologists and decor includes fossils, bones, etc. Fare is simple and offerings are similar for both lunch and dinner: burgers, hot dogs, chicken nuggets. If you enjoyed the character breakfast here in the past, note that it's been discontinued.

Tusker House Restaurant (Africa, Harambe) $$
The food at this restaurant really hits the spot and it's tasty as well as health-conscious. Order up specialities like grilled chicken salad with focaccia bread, rotisserie or fried chicken, or a grilled chicken, ham or turkey wrap. The grilled salmon as well as the fried chicken sandwiches, are also hits. Get a slice of carrot cake for dessert while you settle back and listen to a live African band.

Yak & Yeti (Asia) $$
Specializing in Asian Fusion cuisine, choose from tasty options like miso salmon, stir-fried beef and broccoli, baby back ribs, or crispy mahimahi. For dessert, try the mango pie. African beers and specialty drinks are popular here.

DOWNTOWN DISNEY AREA SLEEPS

Disney's Old Key West Resort $$$$

You'll feel like you're in the laid-back Florida Keys if you stay here. There are 761 studios and villas that have one, two, or three bedrooms. Color schemes and styles of the rooms are done in Key West themes. There's plenty to do here, including biking, boating, shopping, swimming, and tennis. The resort also has a health club and a kids play area. *Info: 407/827-7700.*

Disney's Saratoga Springs Resort & Spa $$$$

Right across the lake from Downtown Disney, this property covers 65 acres once occupied by the Disney Institute. You'll find studios and villas with one, two, and three bedrooms. A couple of on-site restaurants offer breakfast, lunch, and dinner. In addition to a spa, there are loads of activities offered here, including swimming, biking, boating, golf, and more. There's also a health club. *Info: 407/827-1100.*

Port Orleans French Quarter $$$

This resort and the Port Orleans Riverside (formerly known as Dixie Landings) technically function as one resort. Basically, you can have French Quarter or Riverside options. With the wrought-iron features and landscaping, the property draws comparisions to the historic French Quarter of New Orleans. There are 1,008 rooms at the resort and they are located in seven 3-story buildings.

A food court offers several dining possibilities, including the Sassagoula Floatworks & Food Factory where you'll find gumbo and other traditional Creole dishes on the menu. Among recreational activities available are biking, boating, carriage rides, fishing, and swimming. *Info: 407/934-5000.*

DOWNTOWN DISNEY AREA EATS

Bongo's Cuban Cafe (West Side) $$

Created by singer Gloria Estefan, the menu focuses on Cuban and Latin American cuisine. Specialties include black bean soup, deep-fried plaintain chips and steak topped with onions and flan. A favorite is the "La Habana," lobster, shrimp, scallops, squid, clams, and mussels in a piquant creole sauce. There's Latin music on Friday and Saturday. Don't worry, you can't miss the restaurant - it's located inside a building shaped like a pineapple.

Cap'N Jack's Restaurant (Marketplace) $$

This waterfront eatery is where you can go to get your fill of oysters. Or maybe quench your thirst with a huge strawberry margarita made with strawberry tequila, one of the house specials. For lunch or dinner, order a seafood or pasta dish; even the appetizers are filling - try the crab cakes or clam chowder.

Cooke's of Dublin (The Landing) $$

If you haven't had fish and chips lately, step into Cooke's and enjoy the dish here. But don't think you'll have any luck getting the recipe - it's a Cooke family secret. Other menu choices include beef and lamb pie or battered chicken on a skewer.

Earl of Sandwich (Marketplace) $

Yep - this eatery specializes in sandwiches. Your choices include hot and cold freshly prepared sandwiches with original sauces and spreads. Breakfast sandwiches are available too.

Fulton's Crab House $$

If you enjoy seafood then you'll probably love this restaurant. A traditional seafood house, the eatery occupies a three-deck riverboat that's permanently docked on the western edge of Village Lake. The menu changes daily to reflect new arrivals but it usually includes several types of fish, crabs, and oysters as well as lobster, grilled chicken, steaks, grilled vegetables, and combo platters. For sides, go for grilled asparagus or mashed potatoes. While dining, enjoy the nautical-themed interior. Seating on the deck is often available. Reservations suggested.

House of Blues (West Side) $$

Yes, this is the nightclub that Blues Brother Dan Aykroyd helped launch and it doubles as a Mississippi Delta-inspired dining spot. You can't go wrong with the jambalaya or etouffee. A terrific gospel brunch is presented on Sundays. Reservations suggested.

Planet Hollywood (West Side) $$

Built on three levels, the restaurant is absolutely packed with classic movie and television memorabilia. The menu has quite a variety, such as sandwiches, burgers, pasta dishes, fajitas, pizzas, salads. Favorites include the blackened shrimp and the pasta primavera. While waiting for your dinner, enjoy gazing at all of the memorabilia on the walls.

Raglan Road (Pleasure Island) $

A charming, lively eatery you'll find traditional Irish cuisine served up in surroundings that include lovely antiques and live entertainment. Kevin Dundon, one of Ireland's most well-known chefs, created the menu. In keeping with the Irish theme, there are also plenty of spirits! Reservations suggested.

T-Rex: A Prehistoric Family Adventure (Marketplace) $

A new restaurant, this one will be a hit with the kids and has an atmosphere - and menu - that will likely please the entire family. Waterfalls, geysers, and realistic-looking dinosaurs are all draws. But the cuisine also pulls in the crowds. Jurassic Salad, anyone? How about Prehistoric Pot Pie? The names of dishes, along with the decor, will keep little ones entertained while waiting for the meal to arrive. Choices include seafood, steaks, soup, pasta, and sandwiches.

Wolfgang Puck Cafe (West Side) $$

Among the specialities here are gourmet pizzas, rotisserie chicken, and Thai chicken satay pastas with fresh vegetables. There's also a terrific sushi bar. Reservations suggested.

WALT DISNEY WORLD HOTELS BEST EATS

Artist Point (Wildnerness Lodge) $$

For the eclectic diner who enjoys a creative menu, there's buffalo and venison. But you can also order up traditional fare like beef or chicken. Try some of the signature dishes, like berry cobbler or cedar plank salmon. The casual, rustic setting of this eatery is appealing and comfortable.

Big River Grille & Brewing Works (BoardWalk) $$

The sandwiches and salads here are just fine and there are other choices on the menu like veal meatloaf. But it's the ambiance and the chance to sample specialty ales and new beers that really brings people to the eatery.

Bluezoo (Dolphin Resort) $$$

This upscale seafood restaurant, brainchild of celebrity chef Todd English, is an ideal choice if you plan to have a night out without the kids. You can't go wrong with the teppan-seared jumbo sea scallops for an appetizer. Favorite entrees include butter-poached Maine lobster with truffle-potato ravioli or the miso-glazed Chilean sea bass.

Boatwright's Dining Hall (Port Orleans) $$
It can be a bit noisy at this casual dining hall located next to the food court but the cuisine is alright. The menu is touted as Cajun but true Cajuns might be disappointed because there's nothing spicy about the food. Oh, well. Just grab a bottle of Tabasco and you can fix that.

Boma (Animal Kingdom Lodge) $$
Even if buffets aren't your favorite type of fare you should still consider Boma because it has one of the best breakfast buffets in all of Disney. Dig in to pancakes, eggs, sausage, hash browns, bacon, grits, biscuits, pastries, and more. Designed to resemble an African marketplace, this eatery also offers up wonderful fare at its dinner buffet - representing more than 50 African countries and including all types of grilled meats. Reservations required.

California Grill (Contemporary Resort) $$$
You know when you see Disney execs dining here that it's probably good. California Grill, located on the hotel's 15th floor, is considered to be one of the best restaurants in Disney. Enjoy specialties like beef filet with tamarind barbecue sauce, goat cheese ravioli, and grilled pork tenderloin. A favorite dessert is the chocolate lava cake. If those aren't enough reasons to visit, consider that you'll have great views of Magic Kingdom's fireworks. Reservations suggested.

Cape May Cafe (Beach Club) $$
Hit the all-you-can-eat clambake in the evenings. Get your fill of clams, shrimp, chicken, mussels, chowder, and potatoes. There's also a character breakfast buffet every morning.

Chef Mickey's (Contemporary Resort) $$

This popular eatery has Chef Mickey and his pals as hosts of a buffet-style feast. The morning meal is classic American favorites and the evening buffet has standards like roast beef, chicken, and pasta. Kids flock to the sundae bar. The monorail passes above the restaurant and life-size illustrations of Disney characters fill the room.

Citrico's (Grand Floridian) $$$

Upscale and specializing in southern French cuisine, partake of offerings such as sauteed tiger shrimp with ziti, artichokes, bell peppers, and roasted garlic in a spicy wine sauce. While dining, enjoy a stunning view of the Seven Seas Lagoon.

End Zone, Intermission, and World Premiere (All-Star Resorts) $

The food courts in each of these resorts - the End Zone in Stadium Hall at All-Star Sports resort; Intermission in Melody Hall at All-Star Music resort; and World Premiere in Cinema Hall at All-Star Movies resort - all offer about the same type of fare. Selections include burgers, hot dogs, sandwiches, pizza, salads, and ice cream.

ESPN Club (BoardWalk) $

A sports bar and family restaurant, there are more than 100 TV monitors here so you definitely won't miss the latest scores. The main dining area looks like a sports arena, with a basketball-court hardwood floor and a giant scoreboard that projects the big game of the day. Cuisine includes standards like wings, burgers, sandwiches, and salads. Full bar.

Flying Fish Cafe (BoardWalk) $$$
Seafood is obviously the specialty here and a favorite entree is the potato-wrapped yellow-tail snapper. Steaks are also offered and there are plenty of desserts to choose from. Seating is available at the chef's counter, giving you a good view of the action.

Garden Grove (Swan Resort) $$
Enjoy a park-like setting at this eatery that offers buffets for breakfast and dinner. Lunch is a la carte. Disney characters are here for dinner and make appearances at breakfast on Saturday and Sunday morning. Reservations suggested.

Grand Floridian Cafe (Grand Floridian) $$
The menu can vary quite a bit here but selections have included burgers, sandwiches, pastries, salads, and vegetarian choices.

Il Mulino New York Trattoria (Swan Resort) $$$
Enjoy upscale Italian cuisine in a trattoria setting. The seasonal menu features special blends of fresh ingredients from the Abruzzi region of Italy. A favorite is the Gnocchi Bolognese (potato dumplings with meat sauce.) Reservations suggested.

Jiko - The Cooking Place (Animal Kingdom Lodge) $$
A sophisticated eatery offering cuisine with an African touch, with a pretty water and stone garden outside the restaurant. Choose from steak, chicken, seafood, or vegetarian dishes that all feature the unmistakable flavors and spices of Africa. The wine list is made up of South African vintages. Reservations required.

Maya Grill (Coronado Springs) $$
Specialities are steak and seafood with a Latin American flavor. Breakfast, an all-you-can-eat buffet, is popular. Reservations suggested.

Narcoossee's (Grand Floridian) $$$
Located on the waterfront of the Grand Floridian, this casual spot has specialties that vary seasonally but can include grilled lamb chops, Maine lobster, and jumbo scallops. There are also plenty of vegetarian options as well as charbroiled meats and seafood. Reservations suggested.

1900 Park Fare (Grand Floridian) $$
The centerpiece of this restaurant is Big Bertha, a band organ built in Paris around a century ago, and sitting 15 feet above the floor in a proscenium. Characters mingle with guests during breakfast and Cinderella visits the dining room at dinner. Choose from seafood, pastas, salads, a variety of vegetables, breads, and prime rib. Reservations suggested.

'Ohana (Polynesian Resort) $$
It's a family-style, all-you-can-eat feast that includes pork, beef, and and poultry, all roasted on skewers up to three foot long. You don't order from a menu, so just sit back and enjoy as servers deliver course after course. Meats are served with a variety of vegetables, salads, and potatoes au gratin. Dinner ends deliciously, with pineapple-coconut bread pudding served with bananas Foster sauce. Polynesian resort singers often entertain during meals, teaching culture, songs, and hula dancing. Reservations suggested.

Olivia's Cafe (Disney's Old Key West) $$
You'll find an assortment of Key West favorites here, including lots of shrimp dishes and conch fritters. Contemporary Southern fare is also served up.

Sanaa (Animal Kingdom Lodge) $$
A new eatery located in the Kidana Village, its name means "work of art." Perhaps you'll describe the cuisine offered here as works of art as well. Reservations required.

Shula's (The Dolphin) $$$
The specialty here is steak but you can also get chicken and fresh fish dishes. Shula's pays tribute to the 1972 Miami Dolphins, the year coach Don Shula led the team to a perfect NFL season. There are photos all over the eatery, and the menu is given on an autographed football. Reservations suggested.

Shutters (Caribbean Beach Resort) $$
This casual island-themed restaurant serves prime rib, pork loin, lamb chops, and jerk chicken. It's also the place to get that big fruity rum drink you've been craving.

The Wave (Contemporary Resort) $$
Located on the resort's first floor, just off the lobby, the new restaurant specializes in healthy and creative American fusion cuisine. If you want to be bold and try something different, this might fill the bill. Reservations suggested.

Trail's End Restaurant (Fort Wilderness) $
A casual log-walled eatery offers an all-you-can-eat breakfast that includes grits, biscuits, gravy, and even a "breakfast pizza." At lunch, choose from sandwiches, chicken, chili, and a taco bar. For dinner, favorites include shrimp and smoked pork ribs.

Victoria and Albert's (Grand Floridian) $$$$
Put on your fancy clothes, get a sitter for the kids (you have to be over 10 years old to dine here), and prepare to have a lovely evening. Elegant details include Royal Doulton china, Riedel crystal, and Christofle silver. More than just a meal; dining here is an experience. The menu is customized each day and dinner selections include fish, red meat, veal, fowl and lamb. There are choices of two soups, two salads, and luscious desserts, including specialty souffles of fresh berries, chocolate, or Grand Marnier. A harpist plays softly in the background and guests, once they've made their dinner selections, receive a personalized menu as a souvenir. Reservations required.

Whispering Canyon Cafe (Wildnerness Lodge) $$
This casual family-friendly eatery offers all-you-can-eat fare such as smoked barbecued meats with choices of sides and salads. Reservations suggested. See photo below.

Yachtsman Steakhouse (Yacht Club Resort) $$$
Were you expecting the yachtsman to serve fish? Well, this yachtsman actually serves up steak and this spot is one of the premier steak houses in Disney World. Reservations suggested.

6. Disney's Best Shopping

HIGHLIGHTS

Although most people might say they aren't here for the shopping but for the attractions, dining, and entertainment, there sure are lots of folks leaving the parks at the end of the day carrying bags stuffed with goodies. Of those who return to Disney again and again, many have become collectors of things like Disney pins, princess items, Mickey memorabilia, or other collectibles. Others might be hoping to find the perfect Disney souvenir, and we're not talking T-shirts. How about a Tinkerbell cookie jar? A Cinderella waffle iron? Well, whatever you're looking for, if it's Disney-related, you'll probably find it here.

MAGIC KINGDOM

Stop in at **The Art of Disney** on Main Street and check out Disney animation art, which includes hand-painted limited-edition cels, character figurines, lithographs, and much more. You can even catch classic Mickey Mouse cartoons while shopping here. At the **Emporium**, also on Main Street, you'll find thousands and thousands of Disney character products, including lots of princess items, stuffed animals, toys, T-shirts, etc. While you're still on Main, wander into the **Main Street Market House** and pick up whimsical items like Mickey coffee mugs or Goofy chef's aprons.

In Adventureland, load up on pirate items at the **Plaza del sol Caribe Bazaar**, a swashbuckler's dream. Get ships in a bottle, eye patches, pirate hats, Jolly Roger flags, nautical gifts, and more. The **Briar Patch** is a favorite in the Frontierland area. It's where you'll find Magic Kingdom logo merchandise, toys, and lots of character items. Also in Frontierland is the **Frontier Trading Post**, a great place to shop for collector pins since it reportedly has the largest selection of pins in the park. Over in Fantasyland, **Tinker Bell's Treasures** is all about the world of princesses. This is the spot to pick up hats, dolls, jewelry, sparkly dresses, and more.

STROLLING ALONG

Not everyone who visits the Disney parks has children with them but many do. If you plan to park-hop in a single day, you don't have to pay for a stroller twice. Just keep your receipt and show it for a new stroller when you arrive at your next park. Better yet? If you can, bring your own stroller and save a few bucks.

EPCOT

In the **World Showcase**, every country represented has at least one gift shop that's dedicated to the history and culture of that nation's homeland. For example, in **Japan**, pick up a beautiful silk kimono or Japanese toys. Or, in **Morocco**, get a Moroccan tarboosh or fez. How about your own belly-dancing kit? In **Italy**, shop for chic Italian handbags and accessories as well as Venetian beads and glasswork.

Head over to Future World and check out **Mouse Gear**, the biggest Disney apparel store at Epcot (see photo below). Browse for Disney and Epcot logo items, jewelry, character memorabilia, toys, T-shirts, hats, books, and much more. Something to keep in mind is that Mouse Gear usually stays open at least 30 minutes longer than the park does, giving you ample time to find the perfect souvenir of your trip without having to fight the crowds while doing it.

ANIMAL KINGDOM

At **Mombasa Marketplace and Ziwani Traders** (near Kilimanjaro Safaris attraction), look for Africa-themed gifts such as pottery and colorful sarongs, plus plush safari animals, T-shirts, books, and toys. Browse **Creature Comforts** (before you cross from Discovery Island to Harambe) for prince and princess costumes, toys, and clothes.

At **Island Mercantile**, to the left as you enter Discovery Island, load up on trinkets like character pins and keychains as well as adorable Tigger and Pooh backpacks.

Disney Outfitters (see photo above), directly across from Island Mercantile, has unique items like pottery with colorful safari scenes hand-painted by artists from Zimbabwe. In the Asia area you'll find Bhaktapur Market, a small shop that offers toy dragons and plush animals, chopsticks, robes, teapots, and teas.

DISNEY'S HOLLYWOOD STUDIOS

At **Sid Cahuenga's One-of-a-Kind**, an antiques and curios store on Hollywood Boulevard, you'll find high-ticket items like autographed photos by celebrities priced from $75 up to more than $2,500 for a Frank Sinatra-signed pic. You can buy clothing previously worn by your favorite soap opera stars. Also on Hollywood Boulevard is **Mickey's of Hollywood**, a great spot to pick up character T-shirts, hats, sweatshirts, plush toys, books, bags, and more. At **Movieland Memorabilia** on Hollywood Boulevard, shop for stuffed toys, hats, sunglasses, T-shirts, key chains, and other souvenirs.

Pop in to **Legends of Hollywood** on Sunset Boulevard and load up on all of your favorite High School Musical and Hannah Montana merchandise as well as items featuring lots of other Disney Channel shows. At **Sunset Ranch**, also on Sunset Boulevard,

browse for Disney character hats, totes, T-shirts, and more.

DISNEY SPRINGS

In the Marketplace, **Disney's Pin Traders** has a huge assortment of collector pins and various pin-collecting accessories. It's Walt Disney World's most extensive pin-trading center and if you're into Disney pins, you're sure to find something here to add to your collection. At **Disney's Days of Christmas**, the largest Christmas shop on Disney property, load up on Santa hats with mouse ears, candles, Christmas cards, handcrafted ornaments, and more. If you want to deck the halls Disney-style, you're in the

right place. At **Summer Sands**, every day is summer! Shop for colorful surfwear, sunglasses, swimwear, and more from brands such as Tommy Bahama, Quicksilver, and Roxy.

Also in Marketplace, visit P**ooh Corner** and enjoy browsing for plush toys, clothing, and souvenirs - all with a Winnie-the-Pooh theme (see photo below). At **Arribas Bros.**, marvel at gorgeous handcrafted items from Spanish artisans and designers, such as cut-glass bowls and vases, sculpture, and more. **World of Disney** is where you should head to find just about anything Disney-related, from character items (watches, costumes, luggage, etc.) to princess gear. In the Princess Room, kids 3 and up can have their faces painted with glitter makeup, get their hair and nails done, and even try on tiaras. If you have a little princess in your life then you'll want to stop by this spot for sure.

WATER PARKS

At Disney's Typhoon Lagoon, there's a beach shop, **Singapore Sal's**, which has swimsuits, hats, sunglasses, water shoes, souvenirs, and Typhoon lagoon logo products. At Disney's Blizzard Beach, a similar beach shop, **The Beach Haus**, offers swimsuits, T-shirts, hats, sunglasses, beach towels, and more.

7. Disney's Best Entertainment & Nightlife

HIGHLIGHTS

- **The Best of Disney's Parks**
- **Fireworks, Illuminations, Fantasmic, Cirque de Soleil, Hoop-dee-Doo Revue and more!**

MAGIC KINGDOM
Mickey's PhilharMagic
(Fantasyland)

This spectacular 3-D show features popular Disney characters, including Donald Duck, Mickey Mouse, Aladdin, and Ariel. The **eye-popping production has everything** - animation, special effects, nostalgia, and pixie dust. Special touches abound, like splashes of water that sprinkle the audience when buckets and

brooms from Fantasia come to life. Characters appear to be floating right in front of you, so close you could almost reach out and touch them.

Wishes
You'll be mesmerized by this whimsical nighttime show that combines moments from from Disney films with dazzling pyrotechnic effects to create a story-in-the-sky **fireworks spectacular**. Narrated by Jiminy Cricket, the production, which can be seen from anywhere within the park, tells a story about making wishes come true. Tinker Bell makes an appearance toward the end of the show when an explosion of silvery stars bursts from the sky, shimmering their way toward earth, and fireworks in a brilliant kaleidoscope of colors explode in the air.

EPCOT
Honey I Shrunk the Audience
(*Future World*)

Sit back and prepare to get "shrunk" by Dr. Wayne Szalinski (Rick Moranis) when a presentation of his shrinking machine goes terribly awry. The special effects make this **3-D presentation** worth seeing. Everything in the show is larger than life, including

the family cat, and a 5-year-old child. Hope you're not scared of scurrying mice, slithering snakes, or barking dogs!

IllumiNations: Reflections of Earth
(*World Showcase Lagoon*)
Taking place at 9 p.m. daily, this **stunning fireworks, laser, and music show** is a real crowd-pleaser and is a terrific way to cap off the Epcot experience. Lasting 30 minutes, the spectacular show that presents the history of our planet, is visible from anywhere around the lagoon, and the lagoon's fountains are a big part of the elaborate production, too. Additional viewing areas have been added along the section between the Germany and China pavilions.

World Showcase Performers
(*World Showcase*)
You can usually catch live entertainment at each pavilion, often performed by natives of the particular country represented. For instance, lucky viewers might be able to view Moroccan belly dancers, African storytellers, a Mexican mariachi band, a Canadian rock band, and more.

DISNEY'S HOLLYWOOD STUDIOS

Beauty And The Beast
A Broadway-style production, this 30-minute show held in the Theatre of the Stars, tells a story through a memorable cast of Belle, the Beast, Gaston, Lumiere, Chip, and Mrs. Potts. The spirited entertainers, in colorful costumes, sing and dance their way through favorite songs from the animated film *Beauty and the Beast.*

Fantasmic!
Sorcerer Mickey (see photo on page 67) takes on well-known Disney villains like Cruella De Ville and Maleficent in this exciting show of **dancing fountains, lasers, lights, and dazzling special effects**. A crowd favorite, the 25-minute, outdoor nighttime production is held at the Hollywood Hills Amphitheater on Sunset Boulevard, which seats close to 7,000 people.

High School Musical Pep Rally
Presented several times a day, this popular interactive *High School Musical*-inspired song and dance party is high-energy fun. Look for the oversized Sorcerer's Hat on Hollywood Boulevard and you'll find all of the action.

DISNEY'S ANIMAL KINGDOM

Festival of the Lion King
(*Camp Minnie-Mickey*)
You'll enjoy seeing Timon, Simba, Pumbaa, and other favorites in this colorful, high-energy tribal presentation that's a celebration of the circle of life. Set to the music of *The Lion King*, the popular show features dancers, singers, elaborate floats, and acrobats. There's lots of audience participation, so you could end up being one of the stars of the show.

It's Tough to be a Bug!
(*Discovery Island*)
This humorous 3-D show filled with special effects, offers a view of the world from a bug's perspective. So, put on your "bug" glasses and enjoy the advenures of Flix and Hopper. Starring a cast of animated and Audio-Animatronic characters, the show is chock full

of weird sensations, strange smells, and plenty of 3-D fun.

DISNEY SPRINGS

Cirque du Soleil

"La Nouba," the surreal show by the world-famous circus company starts out at full speed and just keeps getting better and better. The awe-inspiring performance is about 90 minutes of amazing acrobatics, choreography, eye-popping costumes, and a thrilling grand finale. A cast of 72 international performers takes the stage and the original music is performed by a live orchestra. The show has a little bit of everything and is both mysterious and comical. The word La Nouba translates to "live it up." If you want to live it up, don't miss this show. The show can sell out so it's best to get your tickets well in advance. *Info: Performances are Tuesday-Saturday, 6 p.m. and 9 p.m. Admission. 407/939-7600.*

House of Blues

The restaurant is known for its delectable southern cuisine and the cool blues it serves up but it's the eatery's concert hall next door where the real action takes place. It has showcased local and nationally known artists - everyone from Aretha Franklin to Journey - and blasted everything from rock to reggae from its stages. It probably has the best live-music venue in Orlando. Cover charges vary and performance times vary but take place most nights. *Info: 407/934-2583.*

Raglan Road

Although all of the dance clubs at Pleasure Island are gone, this authentic Irish pub is hopping, with dancers, storytellers, and musicians as well as an assortment of Irish cuisine and beers, ales, and liquors served from four bars. *Info: Open nightly, 9 p.m.-2 a.m. 407/938-0300.*

DISNEY'S BOARDWALK

Atlantic Dance

A nightclub with no cover charge, this is basically a **Top 40 dance club**. An upbeat spot with a spacious dance floor, there's a huge screen showing videos requested by the crowd and a deejay keeps the music coming. Occasionally, live bands rock the joint. The club serves specialty drinks in addition to traditional cocktails. You must be 21 to enter. *Info: Tuesday-Saturday, 9 p.m.-2 a.m.*

Jellyrolls

At this fun and sometimes boisterous piano bar, comedians do double duty as emcees and play **dueling grand pianos** nonstop. If you name the tune, they can usually play it! Everybody joins in and sings along! You must be 21 to enter this club. Cover charge. *Info: Daily, 7 p.m.-2 a.m.*

DISNEY'S DINNER SHOWS

Hoop-Dee-Doo Revue

Presented at Fort Wilderness's rustic Pioneer Hall, this is one of the liveliest dinner shows in Walt Disney World. While a troupe of performers called the **Pioneer Hall Players** sing, dance and entertain, the audience gets their fill of barbecued ribs, fried chicken, corn on the cob, and strawberry shortcake. There are three shows nightly but the prime times sell out months in advance so it's best to call the resort and make reservations well in advance. *Info: Shows are usually held daily, 5 p.m., 7:15 p.m., and 9:30 p.m., Fort Wilderness Resort. Admission.*

Spirit of Aloha

An outdoor barbecue with South Pacific-style entertainment, this show is entertaining for the whole family. With **hula dancers and fire jugglers**, there's never a dull moment. It's best to make reservations at least a month in advance. *Info: Shows are usually held Tuesday-Saturday, 5:15 p.m. and 8 p.m. Polynesian Resort. Admission.*

8. Orlando's Best Activities

HIGHLIGHTS

Once a quiet town surrounded by citrus groves, the Orlando of today is a thriving tourist mecca, a vibrant metropolitan area offering world-class cultural offerings, off-the-beaten path excursions, and so much to see and do that you'll likely want to start planning a return trip as soon as you wrap up your current visit. Here are a few things to keep you busy after you finish your theme park experiences.

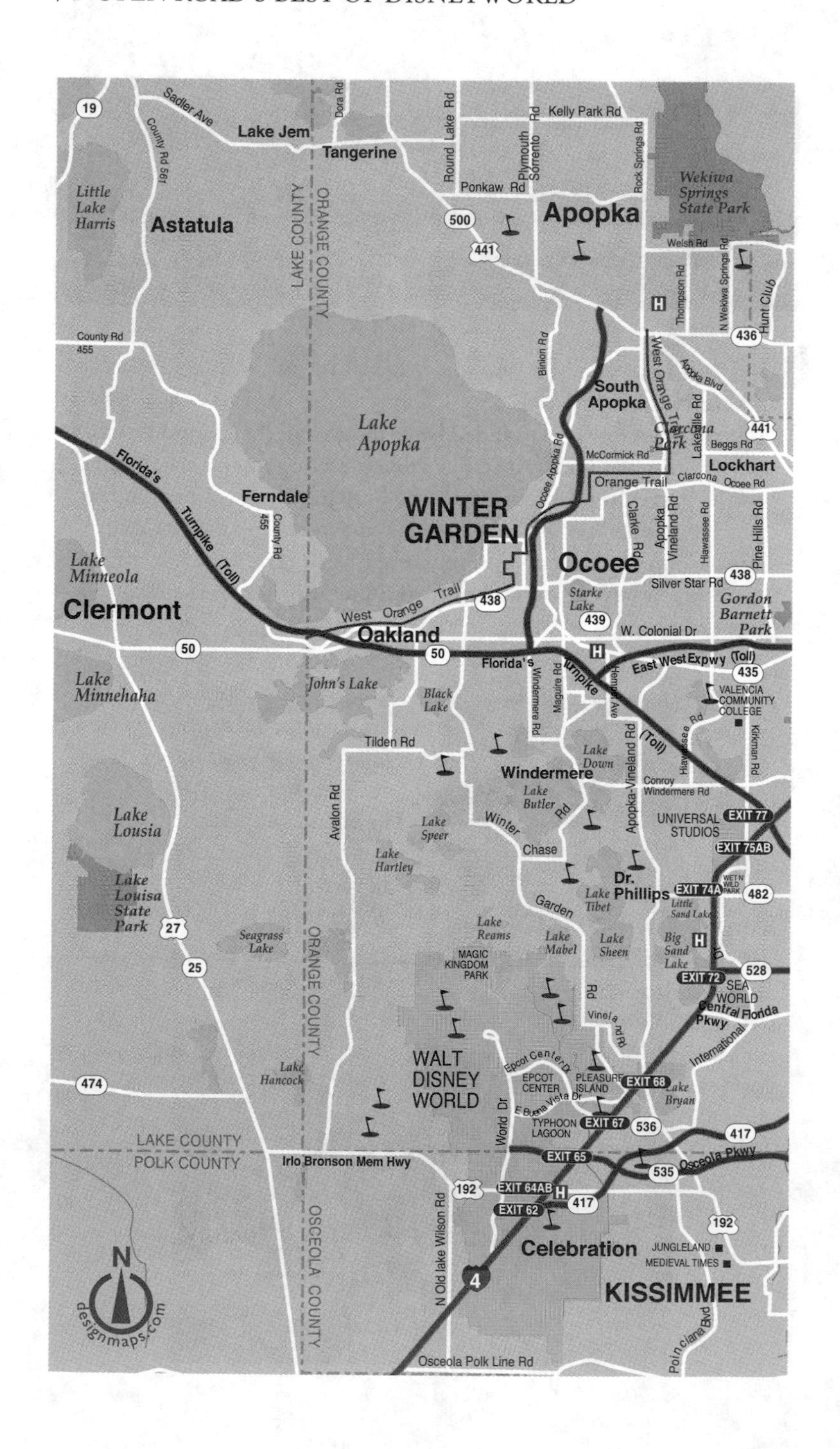

Sadler Ave
County Rd 561
Lake Jem
Dora Rd
Tangerine
Round Lake Rd
Kelly Park Rd
Plymouth Sorrento Rd
Rock Springs Rd
Ponkaw Rd
Wekiwa Springs State Park
Little Lake Harris
Astatula
LAKE COUNTY
ORANGE COUNTY
Apopka
Welsh Rd
Thompson Rd
N Wekiwa Springs Rd
Hunt Club
County Rd 455
Binion Rd
South Apopka
West Orange Trail
Apopka Blvd
Lake Apopka
Clarcona Park
Lakeville Rd
Beggs Rd
McCormick Rd
Ocoee Apopka Rd
Lockhart
Florida's Turnpike (Toll)
Ferndale
Orange Trail
Clarcona Ocoee Rd
County Rd 455
WINTER GARDEN
Clarke Rd
Apopka Vineland Rd
Hiawassee Rd
Pine Hills Rd
Lake Minneola
Ocoee
Silver Star Rd
Clermont
West Orange Trail
Starke Lake
Gordon Barnett Park
Oakland
W. Colonial Dr
Florida's Turnpike
East West Expwy (Toll)
Windermere Rd
Maguire Rd
Hempel Ave
Lake Minnehaha
John's Lake
Black Lake
VALENCIA COMMUNITY COLLEGE
Tilden Rd
Lake Down
Apopka-Vineland Rd
Hiawassee Rd
Kirkman Rd
Windermere
Conroy Windermere Rd
Lake Lousia
Avalon Rd
Lake Butler
Lake Speer
Winter Chase Rd
UNIVERSAL STUDIOS
EXIT 77
EXIT 75AB
Lake Louisa State Park
Lake Hartley
Dr. Phillips
EXIT 74A
WET N WILD PARK
Lake Tibet
Garden
Little Sand Lake
Seagrass Lake
ORANGE COUNTY
Lake Reams
Lake Mabel
Lake Sheen
Big Sand Lake
MAGIC KINGDOM PARK
EXIT 72
SEA WORLD
Vineland Rd
Central Florida Pkwy
International Dr
WALT DISNEY WORLD
Epcot Center Dr
EPCOT CENTER
PLEASURE ISLAND
EXIT 68
Lake Hancock
Lake Bryan
E Buena Vista Dr
World Dr
TYPHOON LAGOON
EXIT 67
LAKE COUNTY
POLK COUNTY
Irlo Bronson Mem Hwy
EXIT 65
Osceola Pkwy
EXIT 64AB
EXIT 62
OSCEOLA COUNTY
N Old lake Wilson Rd
Celebration
JUNGLELAND
MEDIEVAL TIMES
KISSIMMEE
Poinciana Blvd
Osceola Polk Line Rd
N
designmaps.com
19
500
441
436
438
439
50
435
482
528
27
25
474
536
417
535
192
4

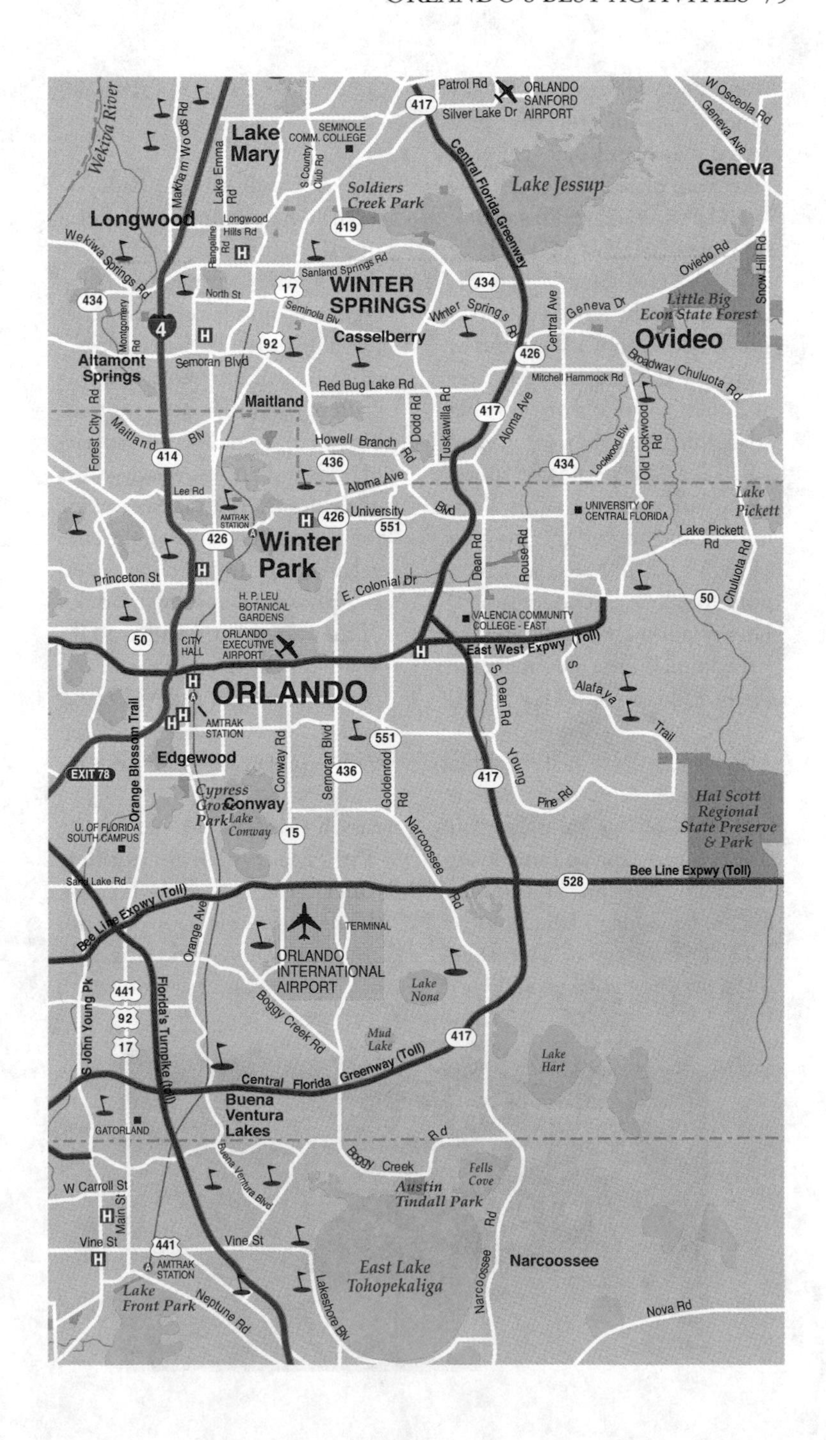
Patrol Rd
ORLANDO SANFORD AIRPORT
Silver Lake Dr
417
W Osceola Rd
Geneva Ave
Geneva
Wekiva River
Markham Woods Rd
Lake Mary
SEMINOLE COMM. COLLEGE
S Country Club Rd
Lake Emma Rd
Soldiers Creek Park
Central Florida Greenway
Lake Jessup
Longwood
Longwood Hills Rd
419
Wekiwa Springs Rd
Rangeline Rd
Sanland Springs Rd
WINTER SPRINGS
434
Oviedo Rd
Snow Hill Rd
434
North St
17
Montgomery Rd
4
Seminola Blv
Winter Springs Blv
Geneva Dr
Little Big Econ State Forest
Central Ave
92
Casselberry
Ovideo
426
Altamont Springs
Semoran Blvd
Broadway Chuluota Rd
Mitchell Hammock Rd
Red Bug Lake Rd
Maitland
Dodd Rd
Tuskawilla Rd
417
Aloma Ave
Forest City Rd
Maitland Blv
Howell Branch Rd
Old Lockwood Rd
Lockwood Blv
414
436
434
Aloma Ave
Lake Pickett
Lee Rd
University Blvd
UNIVERSITY OF CENTRAL FLORIDA
AMTRAK STATION
426
551
Lake Pickett Rd
426
Winter Park
Dean Rd
Rouse Rd
Chuluota Rd
Princeton St
E. Colonial Dr
H. P. LEU BOTANICAL GARDENS
50
VALENCIA COMMUNITY COLLEGE - EAST
50
CITY HALL
ORLANDO EXECUTIVE AIRPORT
East West Expwy (Toll)
S Alafaya Trail
ORLANDO
S Dean Rd
AMTRAK STATION
Orange Blossom Trail
Conway Rd
Semoran Blvd
551
Edgewood
Young Pine Rd
EXIT 78
436
Goldenrod Rd
417
Cypress Grove Park
Conway
Lake Conway
Hal Scott Regional State Preserve & Park
U. OF FLORIDA SOUTH CAMPUS
15
Narcoossee Rd
Bee Line Expwy (Toll)
Sand Lake Rd
528
Bee Line Expwy (Toll)
Orange Ave
TERMINAL
ORLANDO INTERNATIONAL AIRPORT
S John Young Pk
441
92
17
Florida's Turnpike (toll)
Boggy Creek Rd
Lake Nona
Mud Lake
417
Lake Hart
Central Florida Greenway (Toll)
Buena Ventura Lakes
GATORLAND
Boggy Creek Rd
Buena Ventura Blvd
Fells Cove
Austin Tindall Park
W Carroll St
Main St
Vine St
441
Vine St
AMTRAK STATION
East Lake Tohopekaliga
Narcoossee Rd
Narcoossee
Lake Front Park
Neptune Rd
Lakeshore Blv
Nova Rd

Bob's Balloons

Enjoy a one-hour ride over protected marshland that will even take you directly over Disney World if wind and weather conditions are ideal. You meet in Lake Buena Vista at dawn, where the crew take you by van to the launch site. It takes about 15 minutes or so to get the balloon in the air and then you're off on your big adventure. From the **treetop view** you'll see forest land for miles, along with wild boar, cattle, deer, horses, and more. You may go as high as 1,000 feet, at which point you'll be able to see several Disney landmarks, including the Expedition Everest mountain, the Epcot ball, and more.

After the ride, you'll enjoy a champagne picnic brunch. Balloons typically go up in late fall through early spring but the air is usually too hot in summer for the balloons to launch. *Info: 407/466-6380. Fee is around $185 per person; about $100 per child under 12. Prices subject to change.*

Boggy Creek Airboat Rides

Take a fascinating and educational swamp tour on an airboat through the Central Florida Everglades, and see exotic creatures like alligators and bald eagles up close (see photo below). Other critters you might see are otters, blue herons, and various species of birds and turtles. Watch **gators glide across the marsh** seeking their next prey. You might even get an opportunity to take a perfect photo when they jump out of the water to try and snatch a low-flying bird out of the sky for their next meal. *Info: 3702 Big Bass Rd., Kissimmee. 407/344-9550. Admission.*

Busch Gardens

With exotic animals, thrilling roller coasters, and dazzling shows, there's plenty to do at this 300-acre theme park. The park has eight areas, each of which

has its own theme, animals, live entertainment, thrill rides, kiddie attractions, dining, and shopping.

Make sure to check out **R.L. Stine's Haunted Lighthouse**, a 4-D adventure film that combines special effects with multi-sensory surprises.

If roller coasters are your thing, make sure to spend some time at **Scorpion**, a high-speed coaster with a 60-foot drop and a 360-degree loop. *Info: 3605 Bougainvillea Ave., Tampa. 813/987-5082. Admission.*

Cypress Gardens Adventure Park
This attraction bills itself as Florida's first theme park, having opened in 1936. The park did close in 2003 but reopened a year or so later and and now features more than 35 thrill rides, an all-new water ski show, and the **beautiful botanical gardens** that started it all. *Info: 2641 S. Lake Summit Dr., Winter Haven. 863/324-2111. Admission.*

Gatorland
Since Orlando is often referred to as the "**alligator capital of the world,**" this attraction fits right in. Wander the sprawling theme park and wildlife preserve and enjoy train rides, a water park, petting zoo, and about 5,000 animals, including plenty of alligators (a rare blue one is among them), as well as crocodiles,

snakes, and other critters. Shows include **The Gator Jumparoo**, in which alligators jump 5 feet out of the water to retrieve meat from their trainer's hands. At the **Up Close Animal Encounters Show**, around 40 rattlesnakes fill a pit around the show's host. There's also a **Gator Wrestlin' Show** in which handlers go one-on-one with alligators. The **Gator Gulley Splash Park** has several themed splash areas, including one with dueling water guns mounted atop giant "gators" and another in which huge "egrets" have water spilling from their beaks. There's also a petting zoo and an aviary. A free train ride provides a great overview of the park, taking you past an alligator breeding marsh and a natural swamp setting where you can gaze at gators, birds, and turtles. *Info: 14501 S. Orange Blossom Trail, Kissimmee. 407/855-5496. Admission.*

Gulf Beaches

Hitting the beach is an option, especially on those sunny days. Western Pinellas County has more than 30 miles of **white-sand, low-surf, warm-water beaches** that are quite popular. Clearwater Beach, Treasure Island, St. Pete Beach, and Madeira Beach are a few of the standouts.

Kennedy Space Center

If you're ready for a genuine space-age experience, then it's all systems go! Especially if you've always been fascinated by space travel or wanted to be an astronaut. Take an interactive space probe tour, listen to live mission briefings at the Launch Status Center, and take a walk around the outdoor **Rocket Garden** and its collection of eight authentic rockets from past eras. Climb inside the Apollo, Gemini, and Mercury capsules and get a sense of the cramped spaces that the early astronauts' endured. If you've always wanted to touch a chunk of Mars, you can do that, too. Permanent exhibits include Early Space Exploration and the Astronaut Memorial, which is dedicated to U.S. astronauts who died during the course of space exploration. For an extra fee, take the **NASA Up Close tour**, which will take you to sights that are seldom accessible to the public, such as the NASA Press Site Launch Countdown Clock, the Vehicle Assembly Building, the shuttle landing strip, and the 6-million-pound crawler that transports the shuttle to its launchpad. *Info: South of Titusville, on NASA Parkway S.R. 405. 321/449-4444. Admission.*

Mennello Museum of American Art

The museum professes to be Florida's only art museum dedicated to exhibiting **the works of American and self-taught artists**. This unique site also has traveling exhibits, a museum store, and a lovely sculpture garden. The highlight of the small lakeside museum is the permanent collection of vibrant paintings by renowned Floridian folk artist Earl Cunningham. *Info: 900 E. Princeton St. 407/246-4278. Admission.*

Orlando Museum of Art

Nestled in picturesque Loch Haven Park, peruse an extensive collection of works by American artists at this showpiece that's considered one of Florida's cultural gems. Works by **Georgia O'Keeffe**, Thomas Moran, Andy Warhol, Roy Lichtenstein, and others, are on exhibit. The museum's "Art of the Ancient Americas" collection features artifacts circa 2000 B.C. to 1521 A.D., while its African collection showcases such artwork as wooden figures, carved ivory, masks, and ceramics from the Ivory Coast, Nigeria, Botswana, and South Africa. *Info: 2416 N. Mills Ave. 407/896-4231. Admission.*

Ripley's Believe It Or Not! Odditorium

Make sure to visit this attraction if you enjoy all things bizarre. This worldwide chain of attractions displays the unbelievable finds of Robert Ripley's 40-plus years of adventures. Among the displays are: **a mosaic of the Mona Lisa made out of toast**; shrunken heads; a five-legged cow; and a portrait of Van Gogh made from 3,000 postcards. *Info: 8201 International Dr. 407/363-4418. Admission.*

SeaWorld Orlando

At the world's largest marine adventure park, swim with sharks in **Sharks Deep Dive**, go on an underwater adventure with the breathtaking show **Odyssea**, and observe sea lions, seals and killer whales in their special breeding and research habitats. Visit the **Penguin Encounter** and watch penguins strut their stuff. And don't miss the family-friendly **Pets Ahoy** show, featuring a dozen dogs, 18 cats, and an assortment of ducks, parrots, and a pig. The animals peform a series of stunts, which eventually wraps up with a hilarious finale. Stay around until the end and you can get a chance to "meet" some of the stars of the show. At the **Shamu Adventure**, watch the powerful but graceful Shamu as he entertains the crowd and jumps through the air. Want to get splashed? Then, make sure to sit up front. Shamu will not disappoint! *Info: 7007 SeaWorld Dr. 407/351-3600. Admission.*

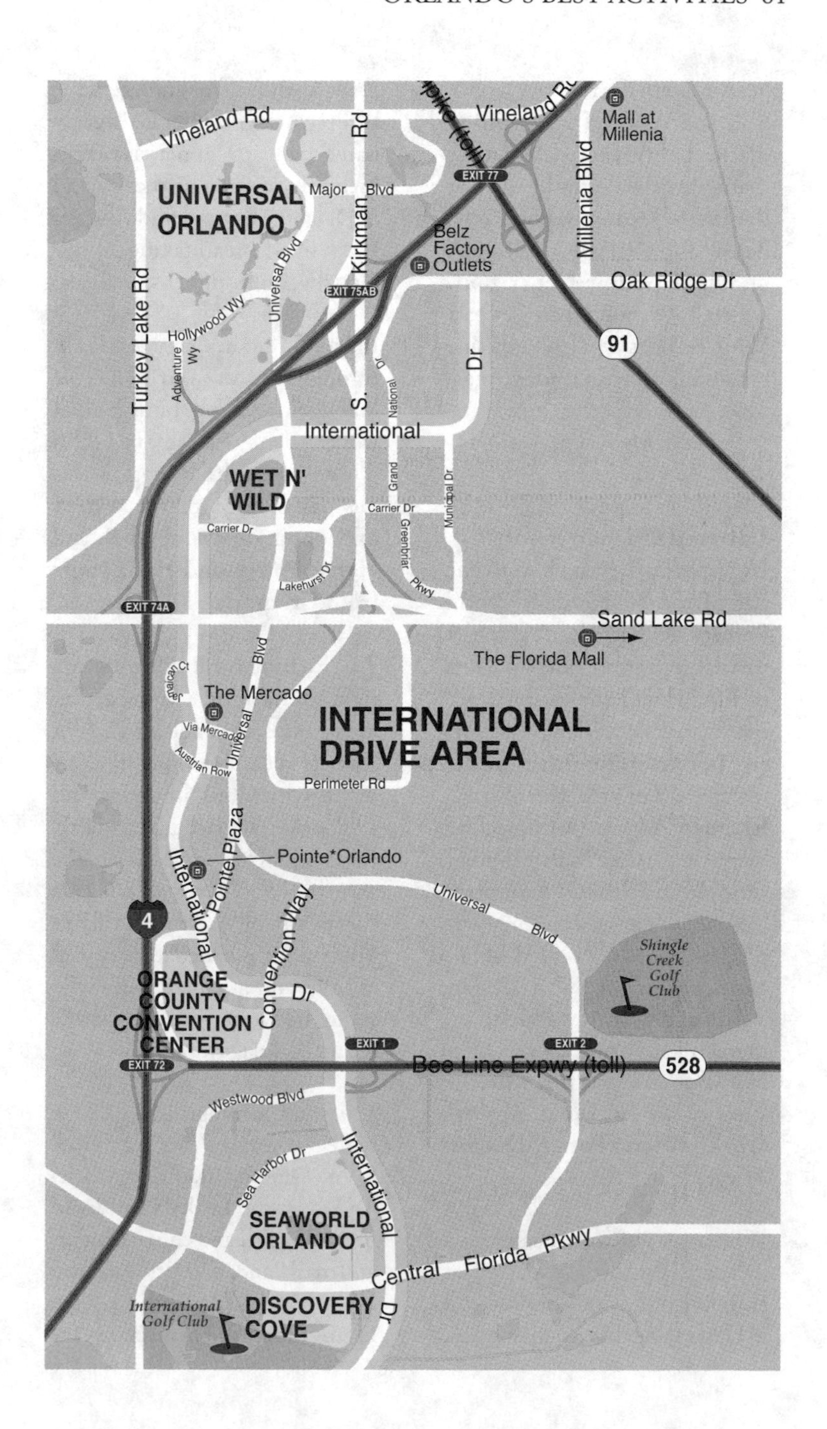
Vineland Rd
Vineland Rd
Mall at Millenia
UNIVERSAL ORLANDO
Major Blvd
Kirkman Rd
S.
EXIT 77
Belz Factory Outlets
Millenia Blvd
Oak Ridge Dr
EXIT 75AB
Universal Blvd
Hollywood Wy
Turkey Lake Rd
Adventure Wy
91
National Dr
International
WET N' WILD
Grand
Municipal Dr
Carrier Dr
Carrier Dr
Greenbriar Pkwy
Lakehurst Dr
EXIT 74A
Sand Lake Rd
The Florida Mall
Jamaican Ct
The Mercado
Via Mercado
Austrian Row
Universal Blvd
INTERNATIONAL DRIVE AREA
Perimeter Rd
Pointe Plaza
Pointe*Orlando
International
Universal Blvd
4
Convention Way
Shingle Creek Golf Club
ORANGE COUNTY CONVENTION CENTER
Dr
EXIT 1
EXIT 2
EXIT 72
Bee Line Expwy (toll)
528
Westwood Blvd
Sea Harbor Dr
International Dr
SEAWORLD ORLANDO
Central Florida Pkwy
International Golf Club
DISCOVERY COVE

Scenic Boat Tour

This is a Winter Park tradition that has been in existence for more than 60 years. From the dock at the end of Morse Avenue, you'll depart for a relaxing, narrated, **one-hour pontoon boat tour**, which leaves hourly, cruises past Winter Park's opulent lakeside estates and travels through narrow canals and across three lakes. *Info: 312 E. Morse Blvd. 407/644-4056. Admission.*

Universal Orlando Resort

Universal isn't even close to the size of the Walt Disney World Resort but that doesn't mean it isn't large, spread out, and lots of fun. Under the umbrella of the Universal Orlando Resort are **Universal Studios Florida**, which is the original theme park; **Islands of Adventure** (the second theme park); **CityWalk** (a dining-shopping-nightclub complex, see photo below); and three on-property hotels. Located about halfway between Walt Disney World and downtown Orlando, there's plenty to keep you busy here. But let's start first with the latest attraction, **The Wizarding World of Harry Potter - Diagon Alley**.

When you visit - you can enjoy delicious British fare as well as authentic food and drink found in Harry Potter books and movies. Prepare yourself for unforgettable thrills when you enter **Gringotts** bank beneath a massive fire-breathing dragon at the far end of Diagon Alley and find yourself swept into a breathtaking, mind-blowing, multi-dimensional ride!

Inside Gringotts you can walk through the bank's lavish marble lobby and watch goblins hard at work. Then, get ready to take a journey through amazing cavernous passageways that lead deep underground as you climb aboard **Harry Potter and the Escape from Gringotts**.

This exciting thrill ride puts you right in the middle of the action as you face the bank's stringent security measures while navigating the perilous underground vaults. You'll encounter Harry, Ron, and Hermione along the way but you'll have to evade the wrath of malicious villains Voldemort and Bellatrix as well as trolls and other creatures who stand between you and a safe return to Diagon Alley.

You won't go hungry here because there's plenty of eats to choose from. Dine on traditional British fare at the **Leaky Cauldron**, including fish and chips, bangers and mash, and, of course, you can enjoy a frothy Butterbeer. Step in to **Florean Fortescue's Ice**

Cream Parlour during morning hours for breakfast items and pastries. Later in the day, enjoy scoop and soft-serve ice cream in a variety of flavors. Multiple kiosks, carts and quick service dining options are also available throughout Diagon Alley.

Now on to some of the highlights of **Universal: Islands of Adventure**. The park has five theme islands which are connected by walkways and the entire area is arranged around a large lagoon.

Among the attractions are **Toon Lagoon**, **Seuss Landing**, **Jurassic Park** and the **Marvel Super Hero Island**. At the Marvel Super Hero Island, the **Incredible Hulk Coaster** will not disappoint but this one isn't for the faint of heart or for small children. The real thrills come when you go into the coaster's first dive, heading straight down toward a lagoon below - at about 60 mph. Speeding along the track, you then start spinning - through seven rollovers. This one's beyond exciting.

Another favorite is the **Amazing Adventures of Spider-Man**. The ride utilizes special effects, 3-D film, moving vehicles, and simulator technology to create a winning combo. In fact, there are times on this one when you'd swear that you really are swinging from Spidey's web.

Over at Toon Lagoon, check out the main street, **Comic Strip Lane**, and you'll notice some favorite cartoon characters - Beetle Bailey, Popeye, Betty Boop, Flash Gordon, Bullwinkle, and lots more. Let your little ones pose under the elevated cartoon balloon captions for those perfect photos. At the Dudley Do-Right's Ripsaw Falls, it's wet-and-wild adventure time with a twisting, up-and-down flume ride through the "Canadian Rockies." If you don't like getting wet on rides, don't go on this one because most riders end up soaked by the end of the attraction.

At **Seuss Landing**, it's all about paying homage to Dr. Seuss. If you'd expect everything to be larger than life and in vivid colors, you won't be disappointed. The designs are whimsical and fun, from the giant red-and-white-stripe hat near the entrance to the colorful sidewalks in various shades of pastel. Seuss characters make frequent appearances, so keep an eye out for the Cat in the Hat, Grinch, and Thing One and Thing Two.

For dining options at Islands of Adventure, you can't go wrong with **Confisco's Grill** since it has lots of options - everything from steaks and salads to soups, sandwiches and pastas.

Universal Studios Florida has more than 40 state-of-the-art rides, shows and other attractions within its 444 acres - stage sets, shops, reproductions of New

York and San Francisco, and soundstages housing themed attractions, as well as genuine moviemaking paraphernalia. There are six "neighborhoods" within the park: **Production Central**, which spreads over the entire left side of the Plaza of the Stars; **New York**, with excellent street performances at 70 Delancey; the bicoastal **San Francisco/Amity**; **World Expo**; **Woody Woodpecker's Kidzone**; and **Hollywood**.

Some attraction highlights include **"Twister, Ride it Out,"** which will put you just 20 feet away from the largest indoor tornado ever created. Debris flies across the stage and signs, a truck, car, and cow also sail by. Even the roof starts to fly away. But all of the destruction is over in about two minutes and you won't even have a hair out of place; and the ride **"Men in Black: Alien Attack,"** where you can zap intergalactic bad guys with laser devices to earn hero points. Depending on your score, the ride ends with one of 35 endings, which range from a hero's welcome to a loser's farewell. This is a fun one as long as you don't believe winning is everything! After the ride, you're in a great location to grab a bite from the **International Food Bazaar**, which has everything from pizza and lasagna to orange chicken and stir-fried beef.

At **CityWalk**, a 30-acre collection of retail shops, kiosks, restaurants, concert venues, and nightclubs, enjoy places like **Jimmy Buffet's Margaritaville**, **Emeril's**, **Pat O'Brien's**, the **Rising Star** (a popular karaoke bar), and the **Red Coconut Club**, one of the newer clubs.

If you dig reggae music, pay a visit to **Bob Marley - A Tribute to Freedom**, which is part-museum, part-club. Modeled after the "King of Reggae's" home in Kingston, Jamaica, there are more than 100 photographs and paintings depicting Marley's life. At the **Hard Rock Cafe** (it's the largest among all the Hard Rock Cafe's), wander around and look

at collectibles like the original lyrics to Paul McCartney's "Let It Be" and Buddy Holly's favorite stage suit. Enjoy dinner but stick around for the show since much of the attraction of this place is the adjoining **Hard Rock Live**. Almost every evening a notable entertainer performs here - from Elvis Costello to Jerry Lee Lewis and lots more. Cover prices for the shows vary. As for the night-clubs, there is a cover charge at all of them but if you invest in a Party Pass (about $12), you gain admission to all of the clubs all night long. Clubs stay open until 2 a.m. *Info: Universal Orlando, 1000 Universal Studios Plaza. 407/363-8000.*

9. Orlando's Best Sleeps & Eats

HIGHLIGHTS

Although lots of people want their lodging to be **within the Disney complex**, there are plenty who don't stay at a Disney property. You have lots of options, including a cluster of hotels that line the mile-long **Hotel Plaza Boulevard** and are often referred to as the Downtown Disney Resort Area Hotels. The hotels, although inside Walt Disney World boundaries, are not owned or operated by Disney. There are other properties as well. We list a selection of both here.

In the last few years, Orlando has become a **food lover's paradise.** Practically every restaurant is overflowing with Florida's natural bounty - from juicy tropical fruits to mouthwatering seafood. Catering to every palate and pocketbook, the restaurants range from small cafes to trendy diners to five-star resorts.

BEST SLEEPS

Best Western Lake Buena Vista Resort $$$

A nice draw of this property is that most of the rooms have private, furnished balconies that offer spectacular views of the nightly Disney fireworks. Although it's not as plush as some of the other Hotel Row properties, it's one of the best bargains for the area. Disney shuttles are available but you can also walk to Downtown Disney in about 10 minutes. There's a restaurant, room service, and a pool. *Info: www.orlandoresorthotel.com. 407/828-2424. 2000 Hotel Plaza Blvd., Lake Buena Vista.*

Maingate Lakeside Resort $$$

A 27-acre hotel complex, this facility has a lovely man-made lake that offers pedal boating and four outdoor tennis courts. Rooms come with two double beds or one king bed. There's a free breakfast for kids 10 and under and plenty of children's activities such as arts and crafts, movies, or miniature golf. There are a couple of pools, a gym, and two restaurants including the Greenhouse Restaurant, home to a freshly prepped breakfast buffet. WiFi is available throughout the resort. *Info: www.maingatelakesideresort.com. 407/396-2222. 7769 Irlo Bronson Memorial Hwy.*

Buena Vista Palace Resort & Spa $$$

This resort (photo on previous page) is located just 100 yards or so from Wolfgang Puck's in Downtown Disney. A nice plus is that all of the rooms have patios or balconies and most offer great views of the Downtown Disney area. There are four restaurants, tennis courts, pools, a gym, spa, and children's

HOTEL PRICE KEY

$	starting below $100
$$	starting at $100-$150
$$$	starting at $150-$200
$$$$	starting above $200

programs. *Info: www.luxuryresorts.com. 407/827-2727. 1900 Buena Vista Dr., Lake Buena Vista.*

Caribe Royale All-Suites Resort & Convention Center $$$
You can't miss the large pink hotel with its palm trees and huge waterfalls. There are plenty of family-friendly features here, such as a huge children's recreation area, including a large pool with a 65-foot slide, and free transportation to Disney sites. Suites are 450 to 500 square feet and have large living rooms with pull-out sofa beds, kitchenettes, and one or more bedrooms. There are four on-site restaurants, tennis courts, laundry facilities, and more here. You should know that it's too far to walk to shops and restaurants from this hotel, though. *Info: www.cariberoyale.com. 407/238-8000. 8101 World Center Dr.*

Legacy Vacation Club $$$
Geared to families, the comfortable one- to three-bedroom suites here can sleep 4 to 10 people. With full kitchens, dining, and living areas, as well as washer-dryers, you get a lot of bang for your buck. The Spanish-style architecture is lovely and the furnished interiors are attractive. There's a small playground and a large outdoor pool.

This property is convenient to the theme parks and Downtown Disney is only about a mile away. There are no shuttles to the parks from this hotel, though. *Info: www.legacatyvacationresorts.com. 407/238-1700. 8451 Palm Pkwy.*

Embassy Suites $$
Convenient to most of the popular attractions, and offering free shuttles to all Disney parks, you're also within walking distance to restaurants and shops from this property. Each suite has a separate living room and two TVs. The atrium lobby, with its rushing fountain, is a lovely spot to enjoy the free cooked-to-order breakfast and evening cocktails. There are two restaurants, a tennis court, pool, gym, and children's programs here. *Info: www.embassysuites.com. 407/239-1144. 8100 Lake Ave.*

Gaylord Palms Resort $$$$

Check in here and you may not ever want to leave. A beautiful, sprawling oasis with amenities galore and picture-perfect surroundings, this property is meant to impress. Inside the resort's huge atrium, covered by a 4-acre glass roof, are re-creations of Florida icons such as Key West, the Everglades, and old St. Augustine. There are extensive children's programs, a large Canyon Ranch spa, great restaurants, and two pool areas. Restaurants include Sunset Sam's Fish Camp, on a 60-foot fishing boat docked on the hotel's indoor lake, and the Old Hickory Steak House. There's not much within walking distance of the resort; on the other hand, there's a free shuttle to Disney. *Info: www.gaylordpalms.com. 407/586-0000. 6000 Osceola Pkwy., I-4, Exit 65, Kissimmee.*

Hilton in the WDW Resort $$$$

A waterfall at the front entrance and a stone fountain surrounded by palm trees makes for a lovely welcome at this resort. The rooms aren't huge but they are cozy and contemporary. Making it more appealing is that many of the rooms on the upper floors offer great views of Downtown Disney, just a short walk way. You'll also find a couple of good restaurants on site as well as programs for kids and a free shuttle to Disney. *Info: www.hilton.com. 407/827-4000. 1751 Hotel Plaza Blvd., Lake Buena Vista.*

Holiday Inn Resort Lake Buena Vista $$

This family-oriented property has some whimsical touches, including a children's registration desk. There's also a small theater where clowns perform in the evenings on weekends. If you stay in the Kidsuites, the little ones will probably love the fact that they get playhouse-style rooms within a larger room (for parents.) The hotel has a restaurant, pool, gym, children's programs, and more. *Info: www.kidsuites.com. 407/239-4500. 13351 Rte. 535.*

Hyatt Regency Grand Cypress Resort $$$$

This lovely, sprawling, top-class resort is close to Disney but not right in the thick of things, which gives a break to families who might want

an afternoon or evening away from the parks. It has much to offer, including a private lake, three golf courses, and miles of trails for horseback riding, jogging, and bicycling. The 800,000-gallon (yes, 800,000 gallons!) pool has a 45-foot slide and is fed by 12 waterfalls. All rooms have a private balcony that overlooks either the Lake Buena Vista area or the pool. Villas have fireplaces and whirlpool baths. There's a great Sunday brunch at the La Coquina restaurant on site. *Info: www.hyattgrandcypress.com. 407/239-1234. 1 Grand Cypress Blvd., Lake Buena Vista.*

Marriott Residence Inn $$

With swaying palm trees and a waterfall near the swimming pool, this property bills itself as a Caribbean-style oasis. But you may be more impressed by the fact that every room has a full kitchen with a stove and dishwasher. There's also an on-site convenience store. Suites include a separate living room/kitchen and bedrooms. The recreation area has both a kids' pool and a putting green. There's a free shuttle to Disney parks. *Info: www.marriott.com. 407/465-0075. 11450 Marbella Palm Ct.*

Nickelodeon Family Suites By Holiday Inn $$$
There are tons of activities for kids at this family-oriented hotel plus a cool Nickelodeon-theme pool. You get a suite with a separate area for the kids, with bunk beds and SpongeBob wall murals and other things of that sort. Kids will probably enjoy the wakeup calls from Nickelodeon stars as well as the character breakfasts. You can choose between one-, two- and three-bedroom suites, with or without full kitchens. There's a free shuttle to Disney sites. *Info: www.nickhotels.com. 407/387-5437. 14500 Continental Gateway, I-4 Exit 67, Orlando.*

Orlando World Center Marriott $$$$
With 2,000 rooms, this is one of Orlando's largest hotels. Every room has a patio or balcony, there are tons of amenities here, and you can even golf at the 6,800-yard championship Hawk's Landing golf course. In the evening, dine at one of seven on-site restaurants, which includes a couple of steakhouses. There are children's programs here, a gym, pool, and more. *Info: www.marriottworldcenter.com. 407/239-4200. 8701 World Center Dr., Orlando.*

Ritz-Carlton Orlando Grande Lakes $$$$
This resort is considered to be one of the best in the Orlando area. Well, it is the city's first and only Ritz after all. When you factor in that it has super-luxurious rooms, spa programs, a championship golf course, and great restaurants, it's easy to see why it's ranked up there.

The rooms and suites here have large balconies, beautiful wood furnishings, and marble baths. The Roman-style pool area has a hot tub and fountains. There are four on-site restaurants, lounges, an 18-hole golf course, pool, gym, spa, concierge, and more. *Info: www.grandelakes.com. 407/206-2400. 4012 Central Florida Pkwy., Orlando.*

Sheraton Vistana Resort $$$
If you enjoy swimming, you've found the right resort - there are seven outdoor heated pools, five kiddie pools, and eight outdoor hot tubs here. Just across I-4 from Downtown Disney, there are lots of on-site recreation options, including tennis. The rooms have kitchens, which could help to save you a few bucks during your trip. The spacious one- and two-bedroom villas and town houses have living rooms, full kitchens, and washer and dryers. This property also has a couple of restaurants, a gym, and concierge. *Info: www.starwoodvo.com. 407/239-3100. 8800 Vistana Center Dr., Orlando.*

Grand Bohemian Hotel $$$$
Downtown Orlando's only luxury hotel, this lovely property has more than 100 pieces of art, including an Imperial Grand Bosendorfer piano (reportedly one of only two in the world.) There's an on-site restaurant, The Boheme, which features Nouvelle American cuisine reflecting French and Pacific Rim influences. The property has a lounge, pool, gym, concierge, gift shop, and more. From here, it's just a short walk to the clubs on Church St. *Info: www.grandbohemianhotel.com. 407/313-9000. 325 S. Orange Ave., Orlando.*

BEST EATS

Bahama Breeze $
The name of the restaurant is a clue to the type of cuisine it serves – Caribbean-style cooking. Favorites include fried coconut-covered prawns and West Indian-inspired baby back ribs with a sweet, smoky, guava barbecue glaze. Finish up with a slice of homemade key lime pie. *Info: 8849 International Dr. 407/248-2499.*

Bubba Gump Shrimp Co. $$
Most people know that this restaurant was patterned after the Forrest Gump movie and that the speciality is shrimp - yes, fried shrimp, boiled shrimp, coconut shrimp - every possible kind of shrimp dish. But there are lots of other things on the menu at this fun eatery as well. The fresh red snapper with lobster butter sauce is a winner and another favorite is the salmon and veggie skillet. But if you're here for shrimp, the large shrimp with crab stuffing is an excellent choice. Huge shrimp are baked in garlic butter, topped with Monterey Jack cheese, and served with jasmine rice. For dessert, patrons rave about the chocolate chip cookie sundae, which includes a warm, fresh baked chocolate chip cookie topped with vanilla ice cream, caramel, chocolate, peanuts, and whipped cream. *Info: CityWalk, Universal Orlando Resort. 6000 Universal Blvd. 407/363-8000.*

Chan's Chinese Cuisine $
Enjoy a far-ranging menu of dim sum and Hong Kong-style dinners here. Delectable dishes include fried chicken with ginger sauce and stir-fried jumbo shrimp with honey walnut sauce. Traditional Chinese paintings line the walls, creat ing a memorable and fun setting. *Info: 1901 E. Colonial Dr. 407/896-0093.*

DINING PRICE KEY

$	under $25 per person
$$	$25-50 per person
$$$	$50-100 per person
$$$$	over $100 per person

Chatham's Place Restaurant $$
If you crave a delicious meal that's also on the healthy side, you might

give this lovely place a try. The chef includes on the menu many herbs, vegetables, and fruits from his own organic farm. For an appetizer, consider the seared ahi and organic rigatoni or jumbo shrimp sauteed in lemon butter. A popular entree is the breast of duck, which comes roasted and thinly sliced with a port wine demi-glaze and fresh blueberries. *Info: 7575 Dr. Phillips Blvd. 407/345-2992.*

Choo-Choo Churros Argentinean Restaurant & Steakhouse $$
This spot is a meat-eater's dream, offering up huge portions of churrasco, the classic Argentinean steak, accompanied by garlicky chimichurri sauce. Other favorites include beef short ribs, sausages, and grilled sweetbreads. *Info: 5810 Lake Underhill Rd. 407/382-6001.*

Christini's Ristorante Italiano $$
This sophisticated establishment specializing in Italian cuisine has special touches like quiet alcoves and strolling musicians strumming soft tunes. Savor delectable specialities like rack of lamb seasoned with herbs and served with balsamic-mint sauce and vegetables or the signature veal chop, broiled, seasoned with sage and garnished with Calvados apple sauce. For dessert, you can't go wrong with a slice of decadent chocolate velvet cake. *Info: 7600 Dr. Phillips Blvd. 407/345-8770. Reservations suggested.*

Citrus Restaurant $
Emphasizing fresh American cuisine with a definitive Latin influence, the menu at this new eatery includes blue crab cakes, marinated skirt steak, bacon-wrapped Maine scallops and yellow fin tuna. *Info: 407/373-0622. 821 N. Orange Ave. Reservations suggested.*

Cuba Libre Restaurant & Rum Bar $
One of the newer restaurants in Orlando, this establishment is part eatery, part dance club. Dinner focuses on modernized Cuban cuisine like grilled skirt steak, honey-mango glazed salmon and mojo-marinated roast pork. But as the evening goes on, tables are cleared, Mojitos are poured, and the massive floor area transforms into a late-night Latin destination complete with floor shows, DJs, and salsa dancing. *Info: At Pointe Orlando Mall, 9101 International Dr. 407/226-1600.*

Del Frisco's $
The specialty here is prime beef, which is aged, never frozen, and cut to order. A favorite with locals, popular choices include filet mignon, the 16-ounce bone-in rib-eye and the 24-ounce porterhouse and lobster. Save room for bread pudding or Mandarin orange cake. *Info: 729 Lee Rd. 407/645-4443.*

Dexter's of Thornton Park $
A casual hang-out for the hip and trendy, this hot spot with funky artwork lining the walls, is where you go to see and be seen and it's also a favorite of locals. The coolness factor may be high but the prices aren't. For something simple but tasty, try the pressed duck sandwich with grilled onions and brie. A more filling dish is the popular shrimp a la provencal sauteed with curry spice, tomatoes, scallions, crushed chilies and homemade pasta. Another favorite is the chicken tortilla pie - a stack of puffy, fried tortillas layered with chicken and cheese. *Info: 808 E. Washington St. 407/648-2777.*

Emeril's $$
This restaurant is the baby of Emeril Lagasse, the Food Network chef who can occasionally be spotted here. Specialties include such fare as andouille-crusted redfish with crispy shoestring potatoes, and grilled beef fillet with bacon mashed potatoes and buttermilk-breaded onion rings. If you're craving New Or-

leans-style favorites like shrimp or red beans and rice, there are all types of variations of those dishes here. For dessert, split the decadent ice-cream parfait: banana-daiquiri ice cream topped with hot fudge, caramel sauce, walnuts, and a double-chocolate-fudge cookie. *Info: CityWalk, Universal Orlando Resort. 6000 Universal Blvd. 407/224-2424.*

Hot Dog Heaven $
A local lunch-time favorite, you'll find authentic Chicago hot dogs and hand-dipped ice cream at this 50s-style cafeteria. Go for the chili-cheese combo or your basic hot dog loaded with saurkraut and the works. *Info: 5355 E. Colonial Dr. 407/282-5746.*

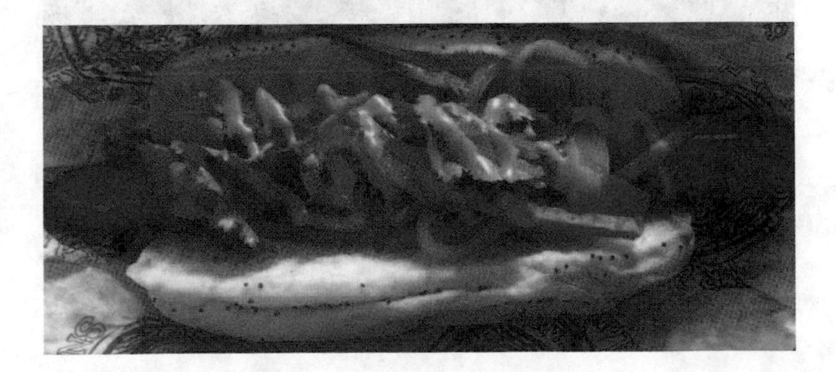

McDonald's $

This is not your typical McDonald's. Once the world's largest McDonald's (there's a bigger one now in Moscow), it still boasts the largest PlayPlace. It also has 60 video arcade games and offers reasonably-priced gourmet fare in addition to its usual menu. Try the panini sandwich, chicken quesadillas, turkey wrap, pasta, or pizza. Open 24 hours, the restaurant also has desserts, like cheesecake and peanut butter pie. You can even get your shopping fix here as you browse McDonald's collector plates, pins, and more. *Info: 6875 Sand Lake Rd. 407/351-2185.*

Ming Court $$

The restaurant bills itself as being all about the art of Oriental cuisine. In other words, dining here is more than just a meal; it's an experience. Situated on two acres and surrounded by lovely gardens, the setting is based on the centuries-old architecture of the Ming Dynasty. You'll have so many appetizers to choose from that you could make a meal from them. Start off with steamed dim sum, shrimp tempura, sashimi rolls, pork dumplings, or any of a dozen or so other choices. For an entree, you can't go wrong with the Indian curry chicken in a flaming wok, which consists of sliced chicken, snow peas, green peppers, Spanish onion, mushrooms and carrots, in curry white wine garlic sauce. *Info: 9188 International Dr. 407/351-9988.*

Ocean Prime $$
It's all about the seafood at this swanky little supper club on Restaurant Row. The shrimp dishes are among the favorites. Listen to a little live music while enjoying your dinner. *Info: 7339 W. Sand Lake Rd. 407/781-4880. Reservations suggested.*

Pho 88 $
With more than 143 menu items, including lots of variations of pho, a soup that is the Vietnamese national dish, you're sure to find something to your liking here. Healthy drinks, exotic fruit juices, and unusually flavored puddings add to the meal. *Info: 730 N. Mills Ave. 407/897-3488.*

Roy's Orlando $$
A hot spot for sophisticated diners, chefs blend European techniques with Asian ingredients for an interesting Fusion-style menu. Scrumptious specialities include kabayaki seared sea scallops with wasabi sweet ginger butter, mahi-mahi with roasted macadamia lobster cream sauce, and wood grilled Szechuan spiced baby back pork ribs. For dessert, the dreamy hot chocolate souffle really hits the spot. *Info: 7760 W. Sand Lake Rd. 407/352-4844. Reservations suggested.*

Season's 52 $$
You'll never get bored with the cuisine here because the menu changes every week, which explains the "52" in the restaurant's name. Even though entrees and side dishes vary each week, the creatively-presented selections always include some type of grilled meats, poultry, seafood, or vegetables. As for desserts, you're in the right place if you want to wrap up an excellent meal with just a taste of something sweet. Specialities

include carrot cake with rum raisin sauce and blueberry lemon cheesecake. Desserts come in oversized shot glasses and are filled with just a bite of cake, pie or pudding. *Info: 7700 Sand Lake Rd. 407/354-5212. Reservations suggested.*

The Latin Quarter $$

Cuisines from 21 nations are on the menu here, along with a variety of South American beers. Favorites include churrasco (grilled skirt steak), puerco asada (roast pork), guava-spiced spare ribs, and fried snapper with tomato salsa. Most entrees come with black beans and rice. For dessert, consider the mango or guava cheesecake. *Info: CityWalk, Universal Orlando Resort. 6000 Universal Blvd. 407/363-8000.*

Timpano Italian Chophouse $$

Located on "Restaurant Row," this upscale Italian eatery provides an an appealing ambience with its ornate chandeliers, velvet draperies, and pristine white tablecloths. Begin with an appetizer of black skillet-roasted mussles, with lemon and drawn butter before moving on to an entree of mouth-watering veal marsala, comprised of tender veal cutlets, mushrooms, marsala wine, herbs and diced roma tomatoes. After dinner, wander into the Starlight Lounge and relax in the cozy setting that includes a lake view, baby grand piano, and an indoor fireplace. *Info: 7488 W. Sand Lake Rd. 407/248-0429. Reservations suggested.*

BEST GRAVEYARD & BREAKFAST SPECIALS

Denny's on East Colonial Dr. has the usual breakfast specials and is open 24 hours.

Panino's Pizza and Grill on Orange Ave. is an eatery that's cool in more ways than one. Not only is it open until 5 a.m., making it one of the few restaurants in Orlando for really late-night/early morning dining but it also has more than 14 by-the-slice variations as well as other pizza choices in whole-pie form. The wings are great for those who like their food spicy; they come crispy and doused with hot sauce.

The 5 & Diner on East Colonial Dr. is open 24 hours and you can get a filling breakfast for a few bucks.

BEST CHAIN RESTAURANTS

California Pizza Kitchen dishes up invididual-sized pizza with toppings ranging from spicy Italian peppers to Jamaican jerk chicken. You can also get items like Santa Fe chicken topped with sour cream, salsa, and guacamole. There's usually a line but the wait is always worth it.

Don Pablo's is the spot to grab some hearty chicken enchiladas and beef fajitas. The I-Drive location of this Tex-Mex eatery is in a big, barnlike building.

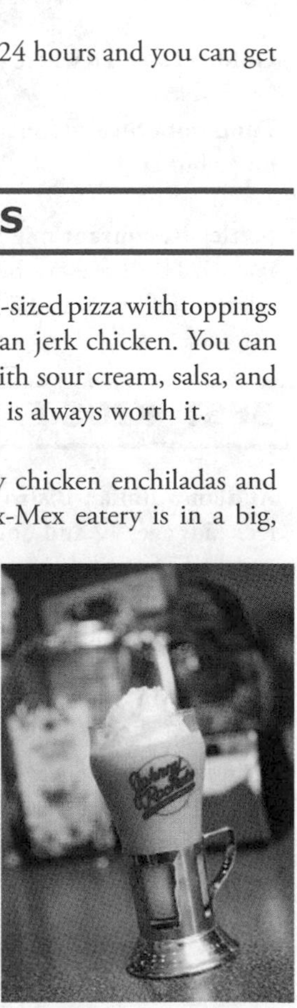

Johnny Rocket's serves burgers and chili dogs in a '50s-diner-style environment. There are branches at the Mall of Millenia, on International Drive, and in Winter Park.

Panera Bread is the place to go for a quick, inexpensive meal like smoked-chicken panini on onion focaccia. You can also grab fresh-baked pastries, bagels, or espresso drinks.

Wolfgang Puck Express is where you can grab a terrific pizza or soup and salad. The two Downtown Disney locations both have walk-up windows.

BEST BARGAIN BUFFETS

If you spend time on International Drive or U.S. 192/Irlo Bronson Memorial Highway between Kissimmee and Disney, you'll see billboards advertising all-you-can-eat breakfast buffets for around $10 or less. It might be a good way to start your day, especially if you plan to spend the day at the parks where restaurants can be pricey. Here's a few to check out.

Golden Corral is where you can fill up on all of your breakfast favorites.

Ponderosa Steak House also has a good selection of breakfast items on its buffet.

Sizzler Restaurant might be where you like to go for steaks but have you tried the breakfast buffet? It's actually pretty good and has a decent selection of breakfast favorites.

BEST 'KIDS EAT FREE' RESTAURANTS

Andiamo Italian Bistro & Grille in the Hilton in the WDW Resort let's kids ages 12 and under eat free from the children's menu with the purchase of an adult entree, Thursday through Sunday evenings. Choices include such fare as chicken fingers and steak fries and Italian favorites like spaghetti and meatballs.

At **Beef O'Brady's,** kids 12 and under eat free on Tuesday nights with each regular paying adult between the hours of 4-8 p.m. Menu choices include chicken fingers, cheeseburger, hamburger, grilled cheese, hot dog, grilled chicken wap, or chicken wings. One Orlando location - Avalon Park in East Orlando; and two Kissimmee locations - South John Young Parkway and West Irlo Bronson Hwy.

Tuesday nights are Kids' Nights at **Gator's Dockside** complete with a clown entertaining and free meals for kids under 12 off the kids menu from 6-8:30 p.m. Limit one free child's meal per paying adult. Lots of items to choose from, including pizza, pasta, wings, mini burgers, chicken fingers, or macaroni and cheese. Several Orlando locations - Dr. Phillips, Vine Street East in Kissimmee, South Orange Blossom Trail, Lake Mary, Winter Springs, and Waterford Lakes.

At **Giovanni's Italian Restaurant**, kids eat free from the kids menu on Monday nights with each adult entree purchased at the Hoffner Avenue location only.

Kids under 12 eat for free from the kids menu on Tuesdays during normal business hours at the **Roadhouse Grill**. Four Orlando area locations - South Orange Avenue, West Vine Street in Kissimmee, West State Road 434 in Longwood, and State Road 436 in Winter Park.

At **Shoney's**, kids under 4 eat free from the kids menu with a paying adult, seven days a week. Apopka Vineland Road near Walt Disney World.

10. Orlando's Best Shopping

HIGHLIGHTS

Orlando boasts excellent shopping choices, from traditional malls like **Artegon Marketplace** (photo below) to outlet centers to unusual places. Whatever your shopping needs, Orlando will not disappoint.

Artegon Marketplace
Previously known as Festival Bay at International Drive, Artegon Marketplace is a shopping mecca that is continuing to evolve as more and more stores are added. It's a long-range project and most of the current anchor stores will remain for at least the next 10 years if not longer. They will gradually be joined by a redesigned skate park, Revolutions bowling alley, the Berghoff German restaurant and a Toby Keith-branded bar and grill. Artegon Marketplace is also known as a place for artists to show off their wares and rents to local handcrafting retailers like **Misty Wheeler-Belin's Florida Soap** and artists such as Robin "R.V." Van Arsdol.

Tenants include jewelers, airbrush artists, skateboard crafters, hot sauce makers, leather workers, and even a glassblowing studio. At **Glen Cove Torch Sculptures**, Central Florida artists hand craft and design sculptures from brass, copper and a variety of metals to create unique sculptures. If you like all things spicy, check out the **Pepper Palace**, which offers a wide array of award-winning sauces, ranging from hot sauces, barbecue sauce, salsas, condiments, seasonings and oils.

Restaurants include **Pizza at Artegon** where you can get a creative and delicious pizza, and **Fuddruckers**, a great choice when you want the perfect burger and a side of fries. *Info: 3 mi. east of I-4 Exit 98 on Lake Mary Boulevard, then 1 mi. south on U.S. 17-92. U.S. 17-92, Sanford. 407/ 321-1792.*

Florida Mall
With more than 250 specialty stores, you're sure to find what you're looking for at this huge indoor mall. The sprawling shoppers' paradise includes such stores as **Dillards**, **Rolex**, **Old Navy**, **Macy's**, **Justice**, **Hollister**, **Hot Topic**, and many more.

There are several full-service restaurants as well as a popular food court that has many options including grabbing a bite to eat from **Nature's Table Cafe**, **Sbarro**, **Greek Urban Kitchen**, or **Five Guy's Burgers and Fries**.

Info: 8001 S. Orange Blossom Trail. (407) 851-6255.

Mall at Millenia

This upscale mecca for shoppers has high-end favorites like **Cartier**, **Chanel**, **Gucci**, **Tiffany & Co.**, and more. Among the 150 shops are also **Anthropologie**, **Neiman Marcus**, and **Bloomingdale's**.

The latest additions here include **Juicy Couture** and **Salvatore Feragamo**. The two-level mall, with its see-through domed ceiling, and plenty of palm trees scattered about, also has eateries galore. We like **California Pizza Kitchen** and **Johnny Rockets**. *Info: 4200 S. Conroy Rd. 407/363-3555.*

Marketplace

This is a convenient site for visitors staying on or near International Drive because it offers all the basic necessities in one area. Not to be confused with Disney's Marketplace, here's what you'll find at this spot: a pharmacy, post office, bakery, dry cleaner, hair salon, 24-hour supermarket, natural food grocery, one-hour film processor, stationery store, and an optical shop. Also in the Marketplace are two restaurants: **Christini's** and **Enzo's**. *Info: Take the I-4 Sand Lake Road exit (Exit 74AB) and head west. 7600 Dr. Phillips Blvd. No main phone.*

Orlando Premium Outlets

Enjoy shopping for everything from **Tommy Hilfiger** and **Fendi** to **The North Face** and **Prada** at this outlet mall. There are more than 110 stores, including **Kenneth Cole, New York Outlet**, **Bebe**, **Coach**, **Guess**, **Theory**, and **American Eagle Outfitters**. You'll also find favorites like **Reebok**, **Timberland**, **Diesel**, **Ann Taylor Factory Store**, **Forever 21**, **Perry Ellis**, and **Lucky Brand Blue Jeans**. *Info: I-4, Exit 68. 407/238-7787.*

Park Avenue Shopping District
More than 100 upscale shops, galleries, and sidewalk cafes dot tree-lined Park Avenue. Wander into **Shoooz** and check out the latest in funky but functional Euro shoes. At **Jacobson's**, browse for chic clothing. If you're looking for something truly unique, stop in at 10,000 Villages, an interesting little store that deals exclusively in fair-trade items.

When your feet (and billfold) need a rest, wander across the street to bucolic Central Park, the heart of Park Avenue. With its lush trees, burbling fountains, and tree-shaded benches, the park makes for a nice respite. *Info: Extends 10 blocks along Park Ave., between Fairbanks Ave. and Swoope Ave., Winter Park. 407/647-9800.*

Pointe Orlando
A nice complex of shopping, dining, and entertainment choices, this oasis for shoppers has more than 60 stores, including the **Armani Exchange**, **Bath & Body Works**, **Tommy Bahama's Retail**, **Hollister**, **Victoria's Secret**, and many more. Surely you won't tire of shopping, but if you do, there are lots of restaurants to choose from if you want to get a quick bite. Among

them are **Maggiano's Little Italy** and **Tommy Bahama Tropical Cafe & Emporium**. *Info: 9101 International Dr. 407/248-2838.*

Prime Outlets Orlando

You'll find a large collection of outlet stores (see photo below) here within two malls and four annexes. Favorites include **Off 5th**, **Saks Fifth Avenue Outlet**, **Michael Kors**, **Polo Ralph Lauren Factory Store**, **Converse**, **Reebook**, and **Nike**. If desired, the stores will ship your purchases anywhere in the United States by UPS. Prime Outlets runs a free trolley between its Design Center, Mall 1, and the Annex. *Info: 5401 W. Oak Ridge Rd., at northern end of International Dr. 407/352-9600.*

11. Orlando's Best Nightlife & Entertainment

HIGHLIGHTS

This chapter includes nightclubs, dinner shows, and spas. Orlando has a great variety of fun things to do at night and during the day, whether you want to dance, drink, take in a relaxing spa treatment, or catch a concert at one of the terrific venues around town (like the **Hard Rock Cafe**, photo below).

BEST NIGHTCLUBS

Chillers, Big Belly, Latitudes
The main attraction on Church Street is a tri-level complex with different bars on each floor. On the ground floor you'll find Chillers, which takes its name from the specialty frozen drinks with funky names it serves. A DJ spins the latest in Top 40 music. On the mid-level, **Big Belly Brewery** provides a **laid-back atmosphere** with big barrels of peanuts as bar food and a cool vibe. **Latitudes**, a rooftop bar that often features live reggae music, boasts a great view of the Orlando skyline. *Info: 33 W. Church St. 407/649-4270. Cover charge.*

CityWalk at Universal Florida
At CityWalk, a 30-acre collection of retail shops, kiosks, restaurants, concert venues, and nightclubs, spend some time at the **Red Coconut Club**, one of the newer clubs here, and catch live music featuring The Herb Williams Band on Thursday-Saturday, and a DJ spinning tunes daily. There's a full bar with signature martinis and an extensive wine list. Sit out on the balcony or mingle with lively crowds inside. At the **Hard Rock Cafe**, enjoy looking at the extensive collection of music memorabilia lining the walls. Grab dinner here but then head to the adjoining **Hard Rock Live** for a concert. Just about every evening a well-known entertainer will take the stage so you're usually in for a treat. Cover prices for the shows vary.

The Rising Star is a fun place if you're in the mood for karaoke. There's a full bar with signature cocktails and a gourmet appetizer menu. Or, catch a performance of the **Blue Man Group** one evening. World-renowned for their live stage shows, **Blue Man Group** showcases their eclectic mix of live music, fantastic percussion intruments, unexpected humor, and more to their performances. If reggae music

excites you, visit **Bob Marley - A Tribute to Freedom**, which is part-museum, part-club. Modeled after the "King of Reggae's" home in Kingston, Jamaica, there are more than 100 photographs and paintings depicting Marley's life. Grab a Red Stripe and jam to some reggae while here. At the groove, dance to the best in 70s, 80s, and dance hits. The club has the latest in sound sytems and special effects, plus three themed VIP lounges. All of the clubs have cover charges but if you invest in a Party Pass (about $12), you gain admission to the clubs all night long. Clubs stay open until 2 a.m. You have to be 21 or older to enter clubs. *Info: Universal Orlando, 1000 Universal Studios Plaza. 407/363-8000.*

House of Blues

Music Hall, a two-story state-of-the-art venue next to the House of Blues restaurant, is the perfect spot to catch a great concert. Top artists like Aretha Franklin and Fiona Apple to Los Lobos and the Foo Fighters have graced the House of Blues stage. If you get hungry, the restaurant offers up specialities like seared shrimp, creole jambalaya, and white chocolate banana bread pudding (it's as decadent and delicious as it sounds!) *Info: Downtown Disney, West Side. 407/934-2583. Cover charge.*

Social

Enjoy live music seven nights a week - everything from **jazz to alternative rock** - while sipping trademark martinis. Some big-name acts, including Matchbox Twenty, played at this joint early in their careers. You can also have dinner here Wednesday-Saturday. *Info: 54 N. Orange Ave. 407/246-1419. Cover charge.*

BEST DINNER SHOWS

Capone's Dinner and Show

This entertaining show takes viewers back to the era of 1931 gangland Chicago, when mobsters and dames were all the rage of underworld society. Your evening starts out in an old-fashioned ice-cream parlor but just say the secret password and you'll soon be ushered right in to **Al Capone's Underworld Cabaret and Speakeasy**. Dinner is an unlimited Italian buffet - lasagna, spaghetti and meatballs, tossed salad, macaroni and cheese, breadsticks, decadent desserts. *Info: 4740 W. Irlo Bronson Memorial Hwy., Kissimmee. 407/397-2378. Performances take place daily, 7:30 p.m. Admission.*

Medieval Times

An extravaganza of sword fights, jousting matches, and other games take place throughout the evening with a supporting cast of **75 knights, nobles, and maidens** not to mention more than 25 horses. Before or after dinner and the show, take a tour through a dungeon and torture chamber or watch demonstrations of antique blacksmith, woodworking, or pottery making. *Info: 4510 W. Irlo Bronson Memorial Hwy., Kissimmee. 800/229-8300. Performances take place daily, 8 p.m. Admission.*

BEST SPAS

Spa treatments are all about the R&R - relaxation and rejuvenation. And vacation is a great time to treat yourself because it may be the only time you have some spare time for pampering. Indulge in an array of massage therapies, facials, aromatherapies, signature services, and more.

Here are some of the places where you can enjoy the spa experience while in the Orlando area.

Grand Floridian Spa & Health Club

Elevate your spirit and get those kinks worked out in style at this elegant spa. Treat yourself to lavish massage therapies, body treatments, facials, and enjoy use of state-of-the-art fitness machinery at this **full-service spa and health club at Disney's flagship resort.** Specialities include aromatheraphy baths and a cooling lavendar body wrap. Manicures, pedicures, and other hand and foot treatments are also available. Prices start at around $115 for a 50-minute massage and about $125 for a facial. *Info: Disney's Grand Floridian Resort & Spa. 407/824-2332.*

Mandara Spa

Relax your mind, body and soul in lush surroundings styled after a Balinese retreat. Offering a **comprehensive array of individual programs**, you're sure to find something - whether it's a massage or body treatment - suited to your individual comforts. Some of the treatments include a deep tissue muscle massage, an oxygen facial, and a body nourish wrap. Prices range from around $120 for a facial to $220 for a body wrap. *Info: Walt Disney World Dolphin Resort. 407/934-4772.*

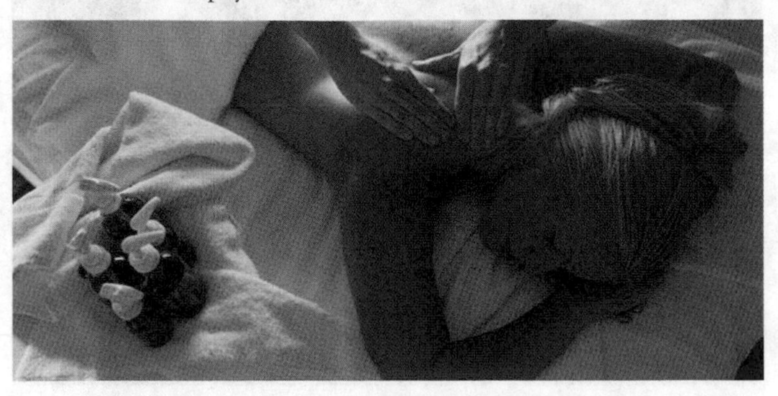

Ritz-Carlton Orlando Grande Lakes
At this lavish spa (see photo below and on page 116) in the Ritz-Carlton, choose from a variety of signature treatments, including the two-hour **Tuscan Citrus Cure**. It starts off with a lemon-crush scrub and lime shower, followed by an aromatherapy massage. Then, you enjoy a soothing hydro-citrus soak in the suite's tub. After that, it's time for a sweet-orange moisturizing body wrap. Afterward, you're treated to a neck or scalp massage. That particular treatment runs about $340 but there are lots of other treatments to choose from, including basic facials or body wraps. *Info: Ritz-Carlton Orlando Grande Lakes. 407/206-2400.*

The Spa at Buena Vista Palace
After hitting the theme parks for several days you may want to stop in and try the cool-mud **Theme Park Leg Relief Wrap** offered here! There are more than 75 other treatments to choose from, including aromatherapy and massage, Swedish, and deep-tissue. Facials, scrubs, and wraps are also available. A favorite is the Golden Door Pineapple Body Scrub, which exfoliates your skin then softens it with oils and moisturizers. The Spa at the Buena Vista Palace hotel is located opposite the Downtown Disney Marketplace, on Buena Vista Drive. A 25-minute massage runs about $75, and facials are around $110. The spa also offers special smassages for kids as

SPA TIPS

Hitting the Spa

To make your spa experience the best it can be, here are a few tips:

- Make reservations for your treatments in advance and make sure to confirm all appointments.
- If you prefer either a male or a female spa therapist, mention your preferences when you make your appointment.
- Don't forget to remove all jewelry before a treatment.
- If you have time, take a shower before a treatment, especially if you've gotten hot and sweaty or have spent a few hours at the theme parks.
- Drink plenty of water after your spa treatments because it will counter any dehydrating effects.
- Be sure to ask about any gratuity (often 18 percent) that might be added to your spa package or treatments.
- Some spas accept reservations up to a year in advance, so it's possible to really plan ahead if you are super organized.
- All resort spas offer bottled water, teas, and healthy snacks.
- With your treatments, you'll also have access to saunas, whirlpools, steam rooms, and fitness facilities.

Men Do It Too!

Spas aren't just for women these days. Many professional athletes visit spas on a regular basis. There are male celebrities that have frequented spas for years. Today, one in four spa customers are men. Some of the spas even offer treatments such as "Zen and the Art of Golfing" or "Men's Spa Escape." Ask your hotel concierge or inquire at check-in about spa treatments that are available.

Pampering For All Ages

Some spas offer mother-daughter packages which include mini facials, massage or body treatments, manicure or pedicure, and more. Inquire at check-in or ask your hotel concierge about what's available.

well as Little Princess manicures and pedicures. *Info: Buena Vista Palace. 407/827-3200.*

The Spa at Disney's Saratoga Springs

Signature services at this spa include the Adirondack and Mystical Forest massages. You can also get **a variety of body wraps and scrubs** as well as aromatherapy, reflexology, sports and Swedish massage and hydrotherapy treatments. Manicures, pedicures, and facials are also available. A 50-minute massage runs about $115 and facials are around $125. *Info: Disney's Saratoga Springs. 407/827-4455.*

12. Practical Matters

Everything you need to know in order to have an amazing time in Orlando - from airport info and tips on getting around Orlando to making the most of your theme park visit and much, much, more - is within the following pages.

ARRIVALS & DEPARTURES

Flying to Orlando

The point of entry and exit for many of the more than 31 million visitors to Orlando is **Orlando International Airport** (*general information: 407/825-2001*). The airport offers direct or nonstop service from 60 U.S. cities and two dozen international destinations. There are more than 35 scheduled airlines and several more charter companies serving passengers who land in Orlando each year. **Rated one of the top airports in the country**, it's a user-friendly facility with lots of restaurants, shops, and centrally located kiosks.

Airport Transportation

Taxi fares begin at around $3.50 for the first mile and $2 for each mile thereafter. Accordingly, the fare from the airport to the Walt Disney World area can run around $50-$60. But if there are four or more people in your group, grabbing a taxi could cost less than taking an airport shuttle.

Another option is **Mears Transportation Group**, which meets you at the gate, helps with luggage, and loads you up in an 11-passenger van, town car, or limo. Vans run to Walt Disney World, International Drive, and along U.S. 192 in Kissimmee every 30 minutes; prices range from about $20 one-way to around $30 round-trip. Limo rates run about $60-$70 for a town car that will accommodate three or four people to around $150 one-way for a limo that seats up to seven or eight people depending on luggage. *Info: 407/422-4561.*

If you are staying at a Disney hotel (except for the Walt Disney World Swan, Dolphin, and Downtown Disney Resort area hotels), you can make arrangements to use **Disney's free Magical Express service**, which includes shuttle transporation to and from the airport, luggage delivery, and baggage check-in at the hotel. You need to reserve ahead because you can't book the service once you've arrived at the airport. *Info: reserve with your Disney hotel when you make your reservation.*

By Train

Amtrak serves the Orlando area twice daily to and from New York City, with several stops along the way. The trip takes about 22 hours and costs around $250 to $330 round trip, coach. *For reservations and information, call 800/872-7245.*

By Bus

Greyhound provides frequent direct service to Orlando and Kissimmee. From either destination, you can take a taxi to your hotel, but first check if your hotel offers shuttle service. *For more info, contact Greyhound at 800/231-2222.*

Rental Cars

All major rental car companies are located at or near the airport. You should probably **rent a car if you're staying at an off-site hotel**, especially if you want to visit attractions or restaurants outside Walt Disney World. But if you're staying at a Disney hotel and spending all or most of your trip at Disney, you can rely on Disney's transportation system for most of your needs.

GETTING AROUND ORLANDO & WDW

If You're Driving in Orlando

The **Beachline Expressway** (also known as Route 528) is the best way to get to the **International Drive** (also known as I-Drive) area and Walt Disney World from the airport. But you need to know that you'll pay around $2 or more in toll charges so it's wise to have some quarters on hand. Depending on the location of your hotel, you'll follow the expressway west to International Drive. You'll exit at SeaWorld for the International Drive area or stay on Beachline to **I-4** and head west for Walt Disney World and U.S. 192/ Kissimmee; or east for Universal Studios and downtown Orlando. You can check with your hotel for the best route.

Walt Disney World has four exits off I-4. For the Magic Kingdom, Disney's Hollywood Studios, Animal Kingdom, Fort Wilderness, and the

GETTING AROUND DISNEY

Get around the Magic Kingdom, Epcot, resort hotels and Disney water parks using the convenient **monorail**, **ferryboat** and **shuttle** network. Shuttle service to Disney's Hollywood Studios, Disney's Animal Kingdom, and Downtown Disney is also available from Disney hotels. If you're driving, remember that each Disney park is separate, with its own entrance and parking facilities.

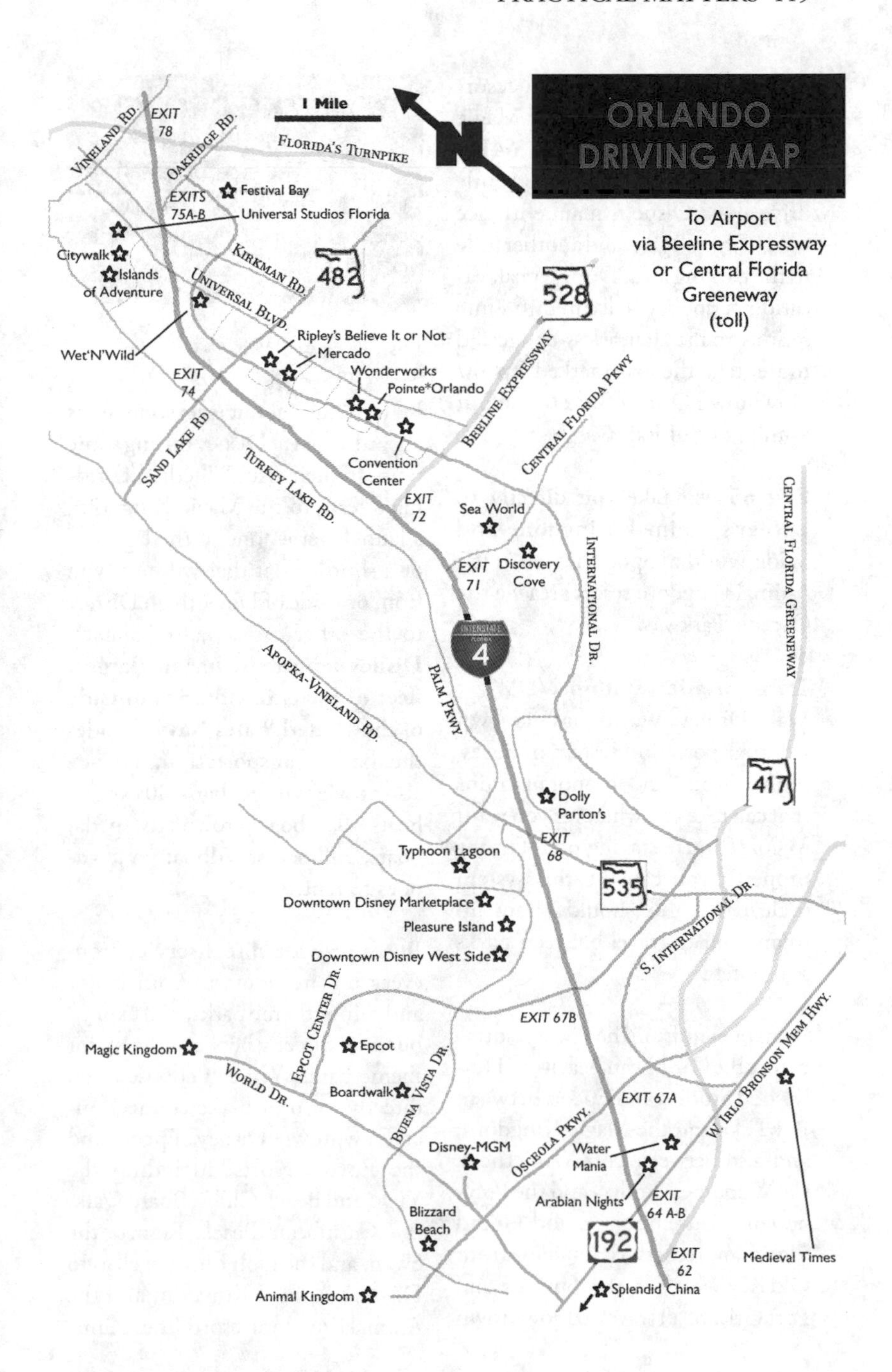
ORLANDO DRIVING MAP
1 Mile
N
To Airport via Beeline Expressway or Central Florida Greeneway (toll)
Vineland Rd.
Exit 78
Oakridge Rd.
Florida's Turnpike
Festival Bay
Exits 75A-B
Universal Studios Florida
Citywalk
Islands of Adventure
Kirkman Rd.
482
528
Universal Blvd.
Wet'N'Wild
Ripley's Believe It or Not
Mercado
Wonderworks
Pointe*Orlando
Exit 74
Beeline Expressway
Central Florida Pkwy
Sand Lake Rd
Turkey Lake Rd.
Convention Center
Exit 72
Sea World
Discovery Cove
Exit 71
International Dr.
Central Florida Greeneway
Interstate Florida 4
Apopka-Vineland Rd.
Palm Pkwy
417
Dolly Parton's
Exit 68
Typhoon Lagoon
535
Downtown Disney Marketplace
Pleasure Island
S. International Dr.
Downtown Disney West Side
Epcot Center Dr.
Exit 67B
Magic Kingdom
Epcot
W. Irlo Bronson Mem Hwy.
World Dr.
Boardwalk
Buena Vista Dr.
Exit 67A
Osceola Pkwy.
Disney-MGM
Water Mania
Arabian Nights
Exit 64 A-B
Blizzard Beach
192
Exit 62
Medieval Times
Animal Kingdom
Splendid China

rest of the Magic Kingdom resort area, take the exit marked Magic Kingdom-U.S. 192 (**Exit 64B**). From that point, it's about a 4-mile drive along Disney's main entrance road to the toll gate, and another mile to the parking area. During peak vacation period's, you'll run into some serious traffic. For a less-congested route, take the exit marked Epcot/ Downtown Disney (**Exit 67**) about 4 miles east of Exit 64.

Exit 65 will take you directly to Disney's Animal Kingdom and Wide World of Sports as well as the Animal Kingdom resort area via the Osceola Parkway.

Transportation Within WDW

Walt Disney World has its own free transportation system of buses, trams, boats, and monorail trains that can take you wherever you want to go. If you're staying on a Disney property, you can use this system exclusively. You should allow up to an hour to travel between parks and hotels.

Boats operate from the Epcot resorts - except the Caribbean Beach - to Hollywood Studios and Epcot; between Bay Lake and the Magic Kingdom; and also between Fort Wilderness, the Wilderness Lodge, and the Polynesian, Contemporary, and Grand Floridian resorts. Launches from Old Key West, Saratoga Springs, and Port Orleans all travel to Downtown Disney, as well.

BEAT THE CROWDS

Try to arrive at the parks early in the day because the lines for rides will be much shorter than they are in the afternoon.

In fact, just about everyone steps aboard a boat at Disney during some point in their visit. Whether it's riding a ferry to the Magic Kingdom, a launch across one of the lagoons, or a shuttle boat that will take you from one side of Downtown Disney to the other. As a matter of fact, **Disney reportedly has the largest fleet of boats in America outside of the United States Navy**. Besides the basic transportation, Disney also provides more than 500 canopy boats, flat boats, rowboats, pedal boats, sailboat, speedboats, and canoes to rent.

Buses provide direct service from every on-site resort to both major and minor theme parks, and express buses go directly between the major theme parks. You can choose to go directly from or make connections at Downtown Disney, Epcot, and the Epcot resorts, including the Yacht and Beach Clubs, BoardWalk, the Caribbean Beach Resort, the Swan, and the Dolphin, as well as to Disney's Animal Kingdom and the Animal Kingdom resorts (the Animal

Kingdom Lodge, the All-Star, and Coronado Springs resort.)

The **elevated monorail** serves many destinations. It has **two loops**. One of them links the Magic Kingdom, Ticket and Transportation Center, and a handful of resorts (including the Grand Floridian, the Polynesian, and the Contemporary). The other loops from the Ticket and Transportation Center directly to Epcot. Before the monorail pulls into the station, the track passes through Future World and circles the geosphere that houses the Spaceship Earth ride, giving you a preview of that attraction. Want to ride in the nose of the monorail with the driver? When you get in line, **ask the gate attendant if you can ride in the nose**. There's usually a maximum of 4 riders. The attendant will ask the next monorail driver if nose seats are available.

Trams operate from the parking lot to the entrance of each theme park. If you parked fairly close you could save time, especially at park closing time, by walking.

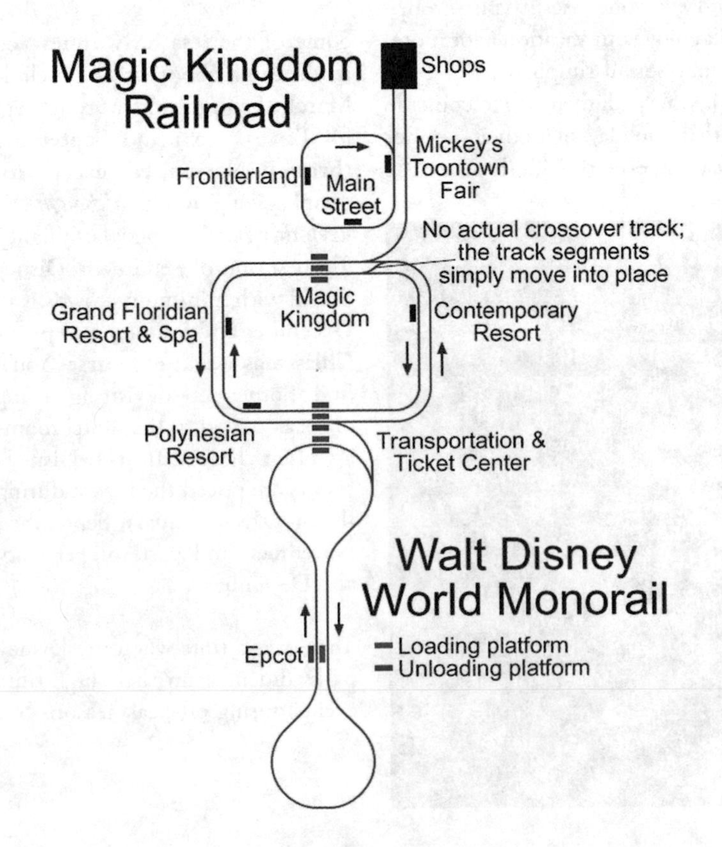

BASIC INFORMATION

When to Visit

You've made the decision that you're taking the family to Disney World and that's great. But one of the most vital things to consider is what time of year is the best time to visit. Don't underestimate the importance of that decision because it could be the difference between a terrific, stress-free visit or a trip that nobody will enjoy. If you decide to go at a less crowded time of year, you'll spend a lot less time waiting in lines and more time on the actual rides, which means you (and everyone else in your group) will enjoy your vacation a lot more. It may sound simplistic. But a lot of people plan their trip to coincide with the holidays or for their summer vacation, even though those are the most crowded times of the year for Disney parks.

EXTRA MAGIC HOURS

If you're a guest staying at a Disney World-owned-and-operated resort, the Swan, Dolphin, Shades of Green, or the Hilton on Hotel Plaza Boulevard, one of the perks is being able to enjoy Extra Magic Hours. The way it works is that one park opens an hour early or stays open three hours late on any given day. If you have a WDW resort ID and a park ticket, you're admitted. You can check with the resort's concierge for a schedule.

Attendance

The biggest crowds of the year are found during the last week in December. It's hard to fathom but more than 75,000 people can enter the parks on these days. And the summer months are nearly as busy. Other times of the year that are really crowded at Disney World are **the weeks of Easter and Thanksgiving**. Another super-crowded time is **President's Week**.

Some of the **less busy times** you might think about visiting include **March through mid-May** (except for Easter week) and **September through November** (except for Thanksgiving week, *although the week after Thanksgiving* is fairly light.) The best time of year to visit Disney World with minimum crowds is in **December and January except for Christmas week, of course**. You'll find another perk of visiting during off-peak periods is that hotel rooms are often cheaper. In fact, Disney's resorts are priced the lowest during the months of January, September, November, and parts of February and December.

There was a time when the Disney parks did not run their nighttime events during off-peak seasons but that is no longer the case. **The Magic Kingdom, Epcot, and Disney's Hollywood Studios end each day with their respective nighttime spectaculars year-round.** So, unless your family simply has no choice but to go during peak-season your best bet will be during off-peak times.

Seasonal Closures

Disney occasionally closes rides and attractions for refurbishment or maintenance and it usually takes place during slower seasons. Before you finalize your trip, **call the theme parks to find out about any planned closures** so you don't show up only to find that a couple of your favorite attractions are out of commission that particular week.

Weather Report

An additional reason that you might want to **avoid summertime visits** to Disney World is that **it can get pretty hot and it rains nearly every afternoon**. It's actually sunny pretty much year-round here, with some occasional rain but temperatures rise quite a bit in the summer months. It's a bit cooler around October-January but temperatures are still pretty mild.

Something else to remember is that, while Orlando is landlocked, it is definitely not immune to tropical storms. Hurricane season typically runs from June 1 through November 30 and although there's no way to predict if or when one will hit central Florida, it's always a good idea to at least consider the possibility.

ORLANDO WEATHER CHART

	Low	High	Rain	Humidity
Jan	48.6	70.8	2.30	56%
Feb	49.7	72.7	3.02	52%
Mar	55.2	78.0	3.21	50%
Apr	59.4	83.0	1.80	49%
May	65.9	87.8	3.55	49%
Jun	71.8	90.5	7.32	57%
Jul	73.1	91.5	7.25	58%
Aug	73.4	91.5	6.78	60%
Sep	72.4	89.7	6.01	60%
Oct	65.8	84.6	2.42	56%
Nov	57.5	78.5	2.30	56%
Dec	51.3	72.9	2.15	57%

Uh-Oh, What If It Rains?

Since some occasional rain is a fact of life here, it's good to be prepared for at least some showers. You can purchase rain ponchos at most sundry-selling stores in any of the theme parks for around $7. But unless you're visiting during the rainy summer months you probably won't need one. Interesting thing about these central Florida thunderstorms - in many cases they are over almost as quickly as they begin. Then, the crowds at the theme parks have usually thinned out and temperatures are even a bit cooler. What's not to like?

If you're checking the weather reports a night before and it looks like the next day might be a rain-filled one, you might consider visiting one of the mostly-indoor theme parks that day, like Universal Studios or Epcot.

ALL RAINED OUT?

Rain showers come along frequently in Orlando but they're usually brief. If it looks like it might rain all day, here are a couple of ways to still make the most of your time: See a movie on one of **AMC Theatres'** 24 screens at Downtown Disney; head to Cirque du Soleil's **La Nouba**; check out **DisneyQuest**, a huge interactive play zone at Downtown Disney West Side; take in an indoor event at **Disney's Wide World of Sports complex.**

SPECIAL EVENTS

Disney World and Orlando are great places to visit at any time of the year, but there are some annual events that are worth arranging your trip around if the events sound like something you and your family would really enjoy.

Epcot's Annual Festivals

A must for epicureans is the **Epcot International Food & Wine Festival**, which takes place Oct. 1 through mid-November. If you can imagine this, the World Showcase's already impressive dining offerings are supplemented by more than 20 international food and wine stands all around the lagoon. You can happily sample your way around the world, one appetizer at a time. There are also demos from top chefs as well as cooking seminars. Additionally, 45-minute wine tastings and seminars are held, with more than 70 wineries participating over the course. The festival also includes a specialty beer garden and the Eat to the Beat Concert Series.

Another popular event is the **Epcot Flower & Garden Festival**, held mid-April through mid-June. The festival showcases elaborate display fields, including exotic internationals around World Showcase. The Flower Power Concert Series at the

America Gardens Theater features folk, pop, and rock acts from the 60s and 70s. Seminars, demonstrations, and Q&A sessions may even be able to help develop some green thumbs.

Cultural, Musical, Artistic, & Ethnic Events
Disney Springs hosts the **Festival of the Masters** (mid-November), a juried art competition. More than 150 artists representing media such as painting, sculpture, photography, clay, and jewelry participate in the open-air festival that features performance art, sidewalk chalkings, folk art, and children's activities. Admission is free. Annual art events include the eclectic **Winter Park Sidewalk Art Festival** (March); the **Winter Park Autumn Art Festival** (October), a juried, community-oriented art show; and the free **Osceola Art Festival**.

If music is your thing, consider downtown Kissimmee (November); and the **Mount Dora Arts Festival** (February), a juried event less than an hour's drive from Disney. Citywalk's **Bob Marley Reggae Fest** (February), which features performances from artists such as Sean Paul and Rita Marley along with Caribbean cuisine and specialty shopping. **Jazzfest Kissimmee** (April) takes place at the Kissimmee Lakefront Park as does the **Kissimmee Bluegrass Festival** (March.) **The Festival of Rhythm and Blues** (February) showcases gospel, jazz, R&B, Caribbean, and African music as part of Black History Month. The **WLOQ Jazz Jams Summer Concert Series** brings monthly performances to Central Park in Winter Park.

In September, two popular celebrations of Christian music are held on the weekend after Labor Day at the Magic Kingdom and Universal Studios, respectively. **Night of Joy** and **Rock the Universe** usually sell out in advance and require a separate admission, as they are held after the parks close to the general public. However, both events' admission will get you into the respective parks after 4 p.m. Night of Joy showcases artists like Mercy Me and Audio Adrenaline, and cost around $45 for one night or around $65 for two nights. Rock the Universe has a harder edge and focuses more on Christian rock (artists such as Michael W. Smith, Third Day, Reliant K.) Prices are similar to admission for Night of Joy but prices for both events are subject to change.

Other cultural events include the award-winning **Fringe Festival** (May), which showcases hundreds of shows from more than 50 groups across 10 days, along with visual art In September, two popular celebrations of Christian music are held on the weekend after Labor Day at the Magic Kingdom and Universal Studios, respectively. Night of Joy and Rock the Universe usually sell out in advance and require a separate admission, as they are held after the parks close to the general public. However, both events' admission will get you into the respective parks after 4 p.m. Night of Joy showcases artists like Mercy Me and Audio Adrenaline, and cost around $45 exibits; **Gasparilla Pirate Festival** (January), where re-enactors have staged pirate invasions of Tampa for the past 100 years; the **Scottish Highland Games** (January), which celebrates the area's rich Scottish heritage with authentic activities, food, music, and games; the **Florida Film Festival** (April), featuring more than 100 films along with seminars, tributes, and a gala; and Orlando's **Gay Days festivities**, which include plenty of music at more than 40 activities citywide during the first week of June.

If you or someone in your group is a car aficionado, more than 150 rare and exotic cars are on display at the annual **Concours d'Elegance** (October) in Winter Park. If you're into motorcyles, **Biketoberfest** brings approximately 12,000 Harley-Davidson enthusiasts to Daytona Beach (October). There's also **Daytona Bike Week** (March), a tradition for 68 years.

Fairs & Festivals

Floridians do enjoy a good party. The same goes for a festival, including these favorites. The **Grant Seafood Festival** (February), **Zellwood Sweet**

Corn Festival (May) and **Florida Strawberry Festival** (March) celebrate some of the area's favorite native foods. Enjoy those foods as they are served up with healthy portions of music, shopping, and rides. Winter Haven's **Florida Citrus Festival** (January) features the **Miss Florida Citrus pageant** and entertainment. But one of the most popular fests is the **Orlando Beer Festival** (November) at Citywalk, drawing around 10,000 people for live festival performances, awards, food from Citywalk restaurants, and more than 150 specialty and handcrafted brews. The Gaylord Palms hosts the **Best of the Summer Florida Fest** (July-August) on weekends over the summer, featuring stunt shows, laser spectaculars, live entertainment, kids' activities, and street entertainers inside the resort's huge atrium.

Sporting Events

Central Florida hosts several major sporting events each year. The largest of them all is NASCAR'S highest-profile race, the **Daytona 500** (March – photo below), held 45 minutes east of Orlando as the culmination of a week-long Speed Week celebration. The **Capital One Bowl** pits the Big Ten and SEC squads against one another on New Year's Day and the **Champs Sports Bowl** features teams from the ACC and Big Twelve in December. Ticket information and prices are announced around the beginning of October.

Another high-profile championship event is the annual **Walt Disney World Golf Classic** (October), this year under new sponsorship from Funai. It entices top name PGA

talent, including past winners like Vijay Singh and Tiger Woods, with $4 million in prize money. And, the **Bay Hill Invitational** (March) has been drawing top PGA golfers for more than 25 years - including Tiger Woods.

CHRISTMAS IN DISNEY & ORLANDO

Magic Kingdom

On selected evenings throughout December, **Mickey's Very Merry Christmas Party** takes place. The park closes to the general public and popular attractions throughout the park remain open. Then, guests enjoy a nightly snowfall on Main Street USA, and entertainment such as stage shows, fireworks, carolers, and the Very Merry Christmas Parade. Santa Goofy greets children on Main Street, families receive a souvenir photo and button, and the delicious aroma of cocoa fills the air. The party runs from 7 p.m. to 1 a.m. and tickets are around $50 for adults, and about $40 for kids 3-9, plus tax.

Besides Mickey's Very Merry Christmas Party, the Magic Kingdom also has a **nightly tree lighting ceremony on Main Street**, as well as special holiday editions of the Country Bear Jamboree and Diamond Horseshoe Revue shows. Other entertainment includes Mickey's Night Before Christmas (in Tomorrowland), and the Celebrate the Season musical revue.

WHEN TO VISIT?

The weeks **between the end of Thanksgiving and the week before Christmas** are generally the least crowded times of the year at Disney World.

Epcot

The **Holidays Around the World** event is a multicultural celebration of the customs, traditions, stories, and songs of the world's various peoples. The walkway linking Future World and World Showcase displays "Lights of Winter," an animated display of illumination synchronized with classic Christmas songs, and each World Showcase pavilion hosts storytellers.

Candlelight Processional, which has been taking place for more than

35 years, is a reading of the Christmas story performed by celebrity narrators along with the Voices of Liberty choir and a 50-piece orchestra. Past emcees have included Gary Sinise, Edward James Olmos, and Jim Caviezel, among others. Performed three times a night at the America Gardens Theater, the Processional is included in regular park admission, and it's advised to show up at least 15 minutes in advance for the best seating.

Disney's Hollywood Studios
Declared a public nuisance in 1994 by the Arkansas Supreme Court, Jennings Osborne's **five-million light Christmas display** was transplanted here from Little Rock. The park is decked out with more than 5 million lights, in the shape of everything from reindeer and angels to glittering Mickey Mouse figures and more. Presented in the Streets of America backlot area, millions of lights "perform" in synchronized motion with music.

Animal Kingdom
Camp Minnie-Mickey is the place to be here, with Disney characters decked out for occasion, plus hands-on fun like making Christmas ornaments and cookies. The **Jingle Jungle Expeditions parade** is a safari-style celebration that takes place daily during the holiday season.

Universal Orlando
At Islands of Adventure, Dr. Seuss's favorite creations come to life in the Whoville-style celebration, **Grinchmas**. Universal Studios has a parade featuring balloons and floats from Macy's Holiday Parade.

Elsewhere Around Town
The **International Drive Fantasy of Lights** features dazzling displays, seasonal activities, and decorations, most of which are free. The **Pinewood Estate** at Historic Bok Sanctuary southwest of Orlando in Lake Wales,

lavishly decorates a 20-room, 12,000-square foot Mediterranean Revital mansion in grand holiday attire (about $15, adults; around $10, kids 5-12.) Bok Sanctuary also has seasonal readings, luminaries, and more. Silver Springs hosts its annual **Festival of Lights** (included in park admission), making this attraction sparkle with holiday cheer.

NEW YEAR'S IN DISNEY, UNIVERSAL & ORLANDO

There are plenty of family-friendly ways to ring in the New Year in Orlando. **Three of the Disney parks are open until 1 a.m.**, with complimentary hats and horns for guests. At the Magic Kingdom, there's extra performances of SpectroMagic and the Wishes fireworks display along with dance parties for kids throughout the park. Epcot has several areas of music - rock, techno, big band, swing, euro, and more. At Hollywood Studios, Fantasmic! is performed three times and the Sorcery in the Sky fireworks cap the night off. All of those festivities are included in normal admission.

> **HOT TIP**
>
> At the end of Main Street, U.S.A., **near Cinderella Castle**, you'll find the **Tip Board**. It's a great source of information on showtimes, other entertainment, and waiting times for attractions.

The Gaylord Palms hosts the **Grande Masque**, a black-tie masked ball produced jointly by the Orlando Ballet, Orlando Opera, and the Orlando Philharmonic Orchestra. The event features an open bar, a five-course dinner, live and silent auction, and a champagne toast. Cost is approximately $295.

HALLOWEEN IN DISNEY, UNIVERSAL & ORLANDO

A pretty tame but fun celebration at the Magic Kingdom is **Mickey's Not-So-Scary Halloween Party**. It's a separate ticketed event (about $45, adult; around $38, kids 3-9.) The party includes five hours of after-house access to rides and attractions, a twice-nightly parade of costumed

SPECIAL EVENTS INFO

Epcot Food & Wine Festival - www.disneyworld.com/foodandwine - 407/824-4321.
Jazzfest Kissimmee - www.kissimmeeparksandrec.com - 407/933-8368.
Night of Joy - www.nightofjoy.com - 407/939-7639.
Gasparilla Pirate Festival - www.gasparillapiratefest.com - 813/353-8108.
Scottish Highland Games - www.flascot.com - 407/426-7268.
Winter Park Sidewalk Art Festival - www.wpsaf.org - 407/672-6390.
Osceola Art Festival - www.ocfta.com.
Mount Dora Art Festival - www.mountdoracenterforthearts.org - 352/383-0880.
Florida Film Festival - www.floridafilmfestival.com - 407/629-1088.
Gay Days - www.gaydays.com - 407/896-8431.
Cours d'Elegance - www.tscevents.com - 352/383-1181.
Biketoberfest - www.biketoberfest.com - 386/271-3120.
Bike Week - www.daytona.bikeweek.com.
Grant Seafood Festival - www.grantseafoodfestival.com - 407/723-8687.
Zellwood Sweet Corn Festival - www.zellwoodsweetcornfest.org
Florida Strawberry Festival - www.flstrawberryfestival.com - 813/752-9194.
Florida Citrus Festival - www.citrusfestival.com.
Orlando Beer Festival - www.orlandobeerfestival.com - 407/224-2690.
Daytona 500 - www.daytona500.com - 904/254-2700.
Funai Classic - www.disneyworldsports.com - 407/835-2525.**I-Drive Fantasy of Lights** - www.internationaldriveorlando.com - 407/248-9590.
Christmas at Pinewood - www.boksanctuary.org - 863/676-1408.
Silver Springs Festival of Lights - www.silverspring.com - 352/236-2121.
Kissimmee Holiday Extravaganza - www.kissimmeeparksandrec.com - 407/933-8368.
Grand Masque - www.grandemasque.org - 407/426-7360.
Halloween Horror Nights - www.halloweenhorrornights.com - 888/467-7677.

Disney characters, trick-or-treating across the park, Halloween fireworks, spooky stories, live music, and more. Make sure you get your tickets in advance as this event does sell out.

The **Halloween Horror Nights** at Universal Orlando, isn't for younger children but if you have teens in your party, they may enjoy it and adults may even get a few frights out of this one. Held at Islands of Adventure, work your way through themed haunted houses and scare zones, including the Field of Screams, Castle Vampyr, the Hellgate Prison, and more. Admission is around $60.

JUST FOR KIDS

Disney's on-site resorts, especially the luxury ones, often have **fun activities for kids** such as pool races or scavenger hunts. **Activity schedules** are usually posted in spots like the pool areas or childcare centers.

SOME MORE BASICS

What Time Is It?

Orlando, like most of Florida, is on Eastern Standard Time.

Where Do You Want to Go?

Avoid that age-old dilemma by deciding ahead of time what you want to do each day. There's no need to map out each minute but making some plans ahead of time can make for a more enjoyable experience. For instance, stay ahead of the crowds by purchasing tickets before your trip; **map out a general daily itinerary** and don't forget to build in a travel-time cushion from hotel to parks. Planning can be fun, especially if you get the whole family involved. And make sure to build in some rest time. Consider starting your day early (it's the best way to hit all of the popular park attractions!), then plan to leave the parks around 3 or 4 p.m., the hottest and most crowded time of day. Rest for a couple of hours at your hotel, have an early dinner, and head back to the parks to watch one of the nighttime spectaculars or to ride a few more rides (lines are usually a lot shorter around closing time.)

A few additional tips: Eat at off times to avoid crowds; buy park-hopper tickets so that you can always go back and see what you've missed another

MONEY-SAVING TIP

Friday and Saturday nights are usually the most expensive at Walt Disney World owned-and-operated resorts.

day; familiarize yourself with all age and height restrictions so that kids won't get excited about rides that they are too small to experience; and consider saving character meals for the end of your trip, when youngsters will have become accustomed to the sight of the characters and won't be scared of them.

Reservations

Make your dining reservations through the **WDW Reservation Center** (*407/939-3463*) before you leave on your trip so you don't have to worry about finding a restaurant every night. Restaurants at Disney book up fast! There's no penalty for not showing up for a reservation, however. You can also make tee time reservations to play at any of Walt Disney World's six golf courses by calling the WDW Reservation Center.

Don't Forget the Sunscreen

It may seem obvious but so many people forget to pack sunscreen. At the first-aid clinic in the Magic Kingdom, sunburn is the top complaint. So, keep some sunscreen with you and apply it often because in Orlando it's generally sunny throughout the year and not just in summer. Pack hats or visors for everyone as well. Painful sunburns could ruin an entire vacation.

Last-Minute Fun

Some people don't know this but you can usually get in line for an attraction at the Disney parks right up until the minute the park closes.

Help is Available

Visit Guest Services or the concierge desks for up-to-the-minute information on schedules, events, parking and shuttle services. Assistance is also available at Guest Relations inside City Hall in the Magic Kingdom, and all other Guest Relations at Epcot, Disney's Hollywood Studios, and Animal Kingdom.

Park Admissions

Visiting WDW is not cheap! **Everyone 10 and older pays adult price**. Also, Disney changes its prices about once a year and without notice. We

ON A BUDGET?

Consider packing snacks such as fruit, cereal, or trail mix for your days at the parks. Snack stands are plentiful but not always cost-efficient. Full-sized ice chests are not permitted. Also, refrigerators are available for free at Disney's deluxe and moderate resorts and for around $10 a day at value resorts.

SAVE ON DINNER!

The average dinner for four at Epcot can run about $100 without wine or beer. Cut that bill in half by visiting the sit-down restaurant of your choice at lunch instead of dinner.

think they realized a long time ago that people are going to go no matter what the ticket prices are. But to be fair, theme parks and attractions all over the United States do the same thing, especially in the economic times we're in. You may save yourself a little bit of money if you buy your WDW tickets as soon as you know for sure that you're going.

Stroller Story

It's obvious that many who visit the Disney parks have children with them. **If you're one of those with small children and you plan to park-hop in a single day, there's no sense in paying for a stroller twice**. Keep your receipt and you can show it for a new stroller when you get to the next park. Another option is to bring your own stroller and save a few bucks.

Buying Tickets

You can purchase your tickets in a variety of ways and you should know that **buying them in advance will save a few dollars** off the price at the ticket booths. You can buy them by phone at *407/934-7639 or at www.disneyworld.com*. You can also get discounted tickets from the **Orlando Convention & Visitors Bureau** at *www.orlandoticketsales.com or 407/363-5871*. In Orlando,you can buy tickets at the **Transportation and Ticket Center** in the Magic Kingdom; at ticket booths in front of the other theme-park entrances; in all on-site resorts if you're a registered guest; at the Walt Disney World kiosk on the second floor of the main terminal at Orlando International Airport; and at various hotels and other sites around Orlando.

All Disney theme park tickets **expire 14 days after first use, unless you've purchased the No Expiration Option**. This includes tickets that are part of a vacation package.

Discounts

Some of the motor clubs offer discounts to Central Florida attractions, including Disney World, so check with your organization. And make sure to ask them about hotel discounts and vacation packages that would include tickets, as well as special benefits within the parks including discounts on meals and nonalcoholic beverages.

civilian with military ID, you can also stay at the on-site Shades of Green Resort for a fraction of what it costs to stay at other Disney resorts.

Packages & Meal Plans
Disney's Magic Your Way basic, premium, and platinum packages can help families budget their money by bundling hotel and theme-park expenses. For around $1,600, a family of four can plan a **six-night, seven-day Magic Your Way Vacation** that includes complimentary transportation from the airport and additional hours in the park. Lower-end package rates offer value-resort accomodtions. All Disney resort guests get free bus, boat, and monorail transportation.

As for meals, if you book a package, you can add on a meal plan for more savings. The Magic Your Way Dining Plan allows you one table-service meal, one counter-service meal, and one snack per day of your trip at more than 100 theme-park and resort restaurants. Another advantage of the plan is that you can swap two table-service meals for one of Disney's dinner shows or an evening at one of the high-end signature restaurants like California Grill.

Have Money Handy
You should be prepared to spend plenty of money and then spend even more money. Theme-park admission is around $75 per day per person. Then, factor in soft drinks, souvenirs, accommodations, meals, and incidentals, and your wallet is going to just get thinner and thinner. But there are ways to save at least a little money during your trip and still have a great time; see below!

PARK-HOP!
Do you want to be a park hopper too? Purchase the **Disney Park Hopper option** and you can visit more than one theme park on a single day.

Save Serious Money!
Here are some important ways to save serious money on your trip:

Consider choosing accommodations with a kitchen and you can do some grocery shopping in a nearby supermarket, saving time and money by eating at least your morning meal in your hotel room; lunchtime prices at most restaurants are lower than the prices at dinnertime; refill your water bottles at the water fountains all over the park; bring your sunscreen, camera, film, batteries, and all other extras you need so that you don't have to purchase them within the theme parks where they are usually very expensive; and visit the parks off-season when lodging rates are lower.

WORD OF CAUTION

Mission: SPACE in Epcot is a great attraction but the ride is not for everyone, and certainly not for anyone prone to motion sickness or sensitive to loud noises or spinning. **It's an intense ride** and there's no backing out after liftoff.

Back to having enough money on hand during your stay:

It sounds so basic and is pure common sense but you'd be surprised by how many people don't bring enough money when they go on vacation. So, make sure you have what you need to get you through the week. Ideally, a credit card, some traveler's checks, and a bit of cash would be a good mix. As for how much you'll need, that depends on what you plan to do while you're here and how good you are at budgeting your money.

Backstage Magic

If you have an extra day and don't have young children with you, you may enjoy this popular tour. This 7-hour excursion takes you on a tour of the Magic Kingdom, Epcot, Disney's Hollywood Studios, and the resort's behind-the-scenes Central Shop area, where repair work is done. The tour departs at 9 a.m. on weekdays and is $199 per person. It's for those 16 and older. The fee includes lunch but does not include park admission, which isn't required for the tour.

Just Hang Up

If you really want to enjoy your time here, put away the cell phone. Of course, everybody has to make - or receive - phone calls. But if you're on the phone or sending texts you might miss some truly special and really fun moments with family or friends. You can always set aside a special time in the day where you can make calls, check messages, or send texts.

Healthy Choices

WDW recently phased out added trans fats and partially hydrogenated oils from food served in its parks and resorts. Most restaurants offer low-salt, low-carb, low-fat, and low-cholesterol choices. Fast-food joints have added items like fresh salads, turkey burgers, and fresh fruit. Healthier dining can be found on

SOAK IT UP!

Whichever **water park** you decide to visit, consider going early in your Disney World trip because many folks save the experience until late in their trip only to find that it was one of the highlights of the whole excursion for their kids.

the kids menus as well. Side dishes might include baby carrots or fresh fruit, with beverage choices of low-fat milk, and 100 percent fruit juice or water.

Best Kids' Events

There are some great WDW activities (besides theme park attractions) that are geared specifically to kids. Here are a couple of our favorites:

The **Wonderland Tea Party** is an hour-long event featuring Alice and her Wonderland friends. Kids make and eat cupcakes, enjoy a light lunch, are treated to a story, and have tea with the characters. It takes place at Disney's Grand Floridian resort, Monday-Friday, at 1:30 p.m. The cost is about $45 per child, ages 4-10. Reservations are required.

We also like the **Islands of the Caribbean Pirate Cruise** in which young buccanneers board a "pirate ship" at Caribbean Beach resort and set sail to search for treasures. The cost is about $30 per child, ages 4-10. Participants should wear socks and sneakers. Check with resort for times that this event is offered. Reservations required.

Romance in the Air

Did you know that Walt Disney World is **one of the most popular honeymoon destinations in the United States**? The resorts are appealing to honeymooners for a variety of reasons, from the white-sand beaches for romantic walks to the fine restaurants offering candlelight dining. Add in the fun of the theme parks, the adventure of the water

Got Cake?

Did you know that you can have a cake delivered to just about any table-service eatery on Disney property? If you want to celebrate a birthday, anniversary, or other special occasion with a cake, simply call the "Cake Hotline" at least 48 hours in advance. *Call 407/827-2253.*

Let's Do Lunch

Meet a Disney Imagineer for lunch at the Hollywood Brown Derby Restaurant on selected days of the week. The cost depends on how many people are in your party. *Call 407/939-3463.*

parks, and the excitement of the nightlife, and it's easy to see why this destination is a draw. You can even tie the knot in evening ceremonies at some parks during seasons when they close early.

The area **in front of Cinderella Castle** in the Magic Kingdom is one of Disney's **popular wedding spots**. Morning ceremonies are offered at Epcot's World Showcase. More than 1,000 couples a year get married at Disney. Some of the things that are offered as part of a wedding package: the bride can ride in a Cinderella coach; have rings brough to the altar in a glass slipper; and invite Mickey and Minnie to attend the reception. *Info: 407/566-7633.*

Sailing Away

Just about everyone steps aboard a boat at Disney during a visit. Whether it's riding a ferry to the Magic Kingdom, a launch across one of the lagoons, or a shuttle boat that will take you from one side of Disney Springs to the other. As a matter of fact, Disney reportedly has the largest fleet of boats in America outside of the United States Navy. Besides the basic transportation, Disney also provides more than 500 canopy boats, flat boats, rowboats, pedal boats, sailboats, speedboats, and canoes to rent.

Good to Know
If there are two performances of the evening parade, the later one tends to draw smaller crowds.

Strange But True
If a park attraction has **two lines, the one on the left is typically shorter**.

All About Dolphins
A 3-hour Epcot program teaches guests all about dolphin behavior as they interact with the dolphins and observe researchers and trainers working with them. Minimum age is 13 and guests 13-17 must be accompanied by a paying adult. Cost is about $150. Park admission is not required or included. Wear a swimsuit; wet suits are provided. Weekdays, 9:45 a.m.

Right on Red
Did you know it's perfectly legal to make a right turn at a red light on roads throughout the state of Florida?

Lost in Paradise
Sometimes travelers get separated from their group or someone may fail to show up at a meeting spot. If that happens, it's good to know that messages can be left for fellow travelers at Guest Relations in any of the four theme parks.

Don't Bring the Kitchen Sink
Travel lightly by leaving things, such as bulky purses, at home. It's safer and more practical in getting around. If you have children in tow, **rent a locker** in any of the Disney parks ($10 per day for large lockers, $8 per day for small lockers).

What Was That?
If you're awakened in your hotel room by the sound of loud booms, don't be alarmed. It's just the space shuttle landing at Kennedy Space Center. The twin sonic booms are produced as the shuttle reenters the atmosphere. The sound can be heard from Cape Canaveral on the coast throughout the Orlando area and all the way to the Gulf Coast.

Meeting Mickey
Your little ones really want to meet Mickey Mouse? Make sure

Mickey's Toontown Fair. Mickey greets visitors there all day, every day.

Gone Fishing
The main difference between the public lakes and the Disney lakes is that you have the option of keeping the fish you catch on the public lakes. Disney has a catch-and-release policy.

Dress for Comfort
Wear comfortable, broken-in tennis shoes or flats. It may seem obvious, but many women end up limping in pain because of their stubborn attachment to strappy sandals and heels.

A Night Out?
In-room child-care service is available 24 hours a day, seven days a week, at all Disney-owned resorts - for a fee of course. Inquire with the concierge at your resort for more info.

Free Admission 'Til 3rd B-day!
Did you know your child can enter the Disney parks for free until his or her third birthday?

This is Cool
At many of the Walt Disney World lounges, you can order food from a neighboring or nearby restaurant's menu. All you have to do is ask.

Lounging Around
If you want to make sure and snag a lounge chair at one of Disney's water parks, make sure you arrive as close to park opening as possible because early birds grab them up quickly.

Other Languages
Many Disney employees are fluent in more than one language. The languages spoken are noted on employee name tags. Most WDW restaurants offer menus in various languages as well. Additionally, free park maps can be found in different languages at the entrance to all parks, as well as at Guest Relations.

Got mail?
Postage stamps can be purchased at all WDW resorts; at City Hall in the Magic Kingdom; at shops near the lockers in Epcot, the Studios, and Animal Kingdom; and at Guest Relations in the Downtown Disney Marketplace.

Thrillsville
You may not know that the phrase "E-ticket ride" is American slang for "the ultimate in thrills." The term comes from the early days of Disney parks when tickets were used for each attraction. E-tickets were reserved for the most exciting rides.

Dinner for One?
If you're traveling alone, many of the finer restaurants at Disney now have counters to sit at - perfect for lone diners.

Valet parking
The cost to valet park a vehicle at any Walt Disney World-owned-and-operated resort is $10 a day. Fees can go up, so it's best to ask when you check in. There is no charge for self-parking for guests at any of the resorts.

Need a Crib?
Playpen-like cribs that will accommodate one child under the age of 3 are available at all Disney resorts. Ask about them when you make your reservation. The cribs are free.

Doing Their Part
Bet you didn't know that many of the benches in Disney's Animal Kingdom are made of recycled plastic milk jugs. So, how many milk jugs does it take to make a bench? It takes 1,350 of them!

Index